A CHRISTIAN DECLARATION ON HUMAN RIGHTS

Theological Studies of the
World Alliance of Reformed Churches

edited by **Allen O. Miller**

Christopher Rose

William B. Eerdmans Publishing Company

Copyright © 1977 by William B. Eerdmans Publishing Company
255 Jefferson Avenue SE, Grand Rapids, MI 49503
Printed in the United States of America

German version: *GOTTES RECHT UND MENSCHENRECHTE*, ed. Jan Milič
Lochman and Jürgen Moltmann, Neukirchener Verlag, Neukirchen-Vluyn.

Library of Congress Cataloging in Publication Data:

Main entry under title:

A Christian declaration on human rights.

    1.   Church and civil rights—Addresses, essays, lec-
tures. I. Miller, Allen O. II. World Alliance of
Reformed Churches (Presbyterian and Congregational).
BT738.15.C47   261.1   77-2796
ISBN 0-8028-1717-3

Contents

Christopher Rose

Foreword

President Carter's forthright stand for human rights at home and abroad has captured the imagination of millions. At a time when "the only universal thing about human rights is their universal denial," there is a growing realization that something has gone awry in human society in the twentieth century, that a virulent spiritual disease has set in upon us which threatens to destroy the fairest hopes for the future. Unlike the revolutions of the eighteenth and nineteenth centuries that were liberating and enfranchising, that extended suffrage in the direction of all, those in our time have been totalitarian, quenching human freedom, confiscating personal goods and often personal identities, and resorting to prison and torture to achieve their ends.

The plight of freedom was very much in the minds of the delegates to the Uniting General Council of the World Alliance of Reformed Churches (Presbyterian and Congregational) when they met in Nairobi, Kenya, in 1970. The invasion of Czechoslovakia had occurred only two years earlier, erasing socialism's emerging "human face," human rights were being systematically stifled in various areas of society on every continent, while dehumanizing political and economic forces were spreading like the tentacles of a giant octopus all over the globe. The Council mandated a study of the Theological Basis of Human Rights, a study that involved many of the member churches of the Alliance as well as a number of special groups and task forces set up to deal with this topic. An initial study draft was prepared by Professor Jürgen Moltmann of the University of Tübingen, who had been a leader in the Nairobi Council, which furnished the background for an ecumenical inquiry into the theological basis of human rights.

The Theological Committees of the organized Areas of the World Alliance in Europe and North America responded to the Moltmann working paper with a series of studies by their members, and the German publication of the European responses has now gone through three printings. *A Christian Declaration on Human Rights* is more than

7

an English edition of the German volume, although it does contain chapters prepared by three European scholars. Professor Allen O. Miller, Chairman of the North American Theological Committee, has added in this book papers by American and Canadian scholars that extend the inquiry into the nature of liberation, the relation of liberation to spirituality, liberation and women's rights, liberation and the black freedom movement, and the relation of liberation to an indigenous theology of the Cross.

The study process of the World Alliance was completed in a Consultation held in London in February, 1976, which was attended by twenty-one theologians from six continents. For this meeting Professor Moltmann produced another working paper, included in this volume, that grounds human rights on "God's right to—i.e., his claim on—human beings, their human dignity, their fellowship, their rule over the earth, and their future." As human beings, Moltmann suggests, we are destined to live before God. Made in His image, we are freed for service to God and to our neighbor, and to serve as stewards of creation. "It is the duty of the Christian faith beyond human rights and duties to stand for the *dignity of human beings* in their life with God and for God." The London Consultation arrived at a consensus statement that is also a part of this document, containing theological guidelines for human rights and some practical implications for the churches and for their relation to the state. Appended are the texts of historic supplementary documents, beginning with the Universal Declaration of Human Rights adopted in 1948 and including the Helsinki Agreement that on August 1, 1975, was signed by thirty-three European states, plus the United States and Canada.

That the churches in the Reformed tradition should give first priority in their study to the theological basis of human rights should not be thought exceptional. Historically, this tradition has championed the cause of freedom and liberation. In his *Institutes* John Calvin included a theology of revolution, and the fact that Calvinist churches were often in the minority in many lands led them to a stance over against monarchies and other ruling powers. During the Bicentennial Year much has been made of the Calvinist contribution to American beginnings and independence. But this was a revolution that was essentially conservative in nature and that tended to be limited to the rising middle class. The challenge today is to broaden the base of liberation to include the poor and the powerless, ethnic minorities, and women.

This volume makes a distinct contribution toward this end by illuminating the theological source of human rights and dignity and by providing basic source materials for study. It contains a summons to all the Churches to join in the crusade to extend the scope of liberation to all mankind.

—James I. McCord
North American Secretary
World Alliance of Reformed Churches

A CHRISTIAN DECLARATION ON HUMAN RIGHTS

1. Human Rights from a Christian Perspective

JAN MILIČ LOCHMAN

I. The Worldwide Struggle for Human Rights

We live in a world echoing in all directions with reports of poverty, hunger, and misery, of exploitation and oppression of great masses of people, of the arrests, tortures, and assassinations of politically undesirable persons, of the abduction and extortion of innocent victims by politically radical revolutionary groups or by greedy robbers, of the suppression of any freedom of expression by dictatorial regimes, including the freedom to confess one's own religious belief—of any number of incidents, in other words, which reveal a frightfully widespread disdain for and degradation of human personhood. In such a world, a deep disturbance of conscience drives us to seek possibilities for the protection of fellow men and women who are being threatened or are being physically and psychologically injured in these ways.

Ludwig Raiser, a Tübingen scholar of constitutional law, briefly sketched in these lines from his essay "Human Rights in a Divided World" the background and context of the growing theological and ecumenical interest in the theory and practice of human rights. This interest has characterized the recent ecumenical movement from the very first—above all the thought and action of the World Council of Churches. Collaborators with the WCC have participated in the elaboration, codification, and defense of the most significant human rights projects, in particular the Universal Declaration of Human Rights (1948) and the Human Rights Covenants of the United Nations (1966).

In the last few years awareness of these human rights issues has intensified. Between the full WCC assemblies of Uppsala and Nairobi there was hardly a session of the appropriate committees in which

Jan Milič Lochman, chairperson of the department of theology, World Alliance of Reformed Churches, is professor of systematic theology at the University of Basel. The translation of this paper from the original German was made by Catherine Keller, Eden Theological Seminary, St. Louis, Missouri.

human rights—especially their widespread violations—were not passionately debated. The urgent phenomenon of racism was given special consideration. Increasingly, however, other forms of violation of human rights, such as the anti-religious discrimination in Eastern Europe, worked their way onto the agenda. The latter was the subject of particularly pointed discussion at Nairobi (1975).

Yet not only the WCC but other church-based movements and organizations as well—such as the Papal Commission *Justitia et Pax*—became involved in the issue of human rights. I need only allude to studies by other world confessional bodies, representing years of careful work. This volume offers the contributions and findings of the study carried out by the World Alliance of Reformed Churches. Moreover, since its full Assembly in Evian (1970), the Lutheran World Federation has also been grappling with the entire complex of human rights issues; no doubt it will soon publish its findings.

The striking ecumenical agreement on the urgency of the human rights problem does not imply, however, an automatic consensus on how to handle this set of issues in ecumenical terms, where to set emphases and priorities, or indeed basically how to understand and to stand up for human rights. In fact, the question of human rights poses itself to us "in a divided world." There is often talk today of the "three worlds": the Western (capitalistic), the Eastern (socialistic), and the Third World of the developing nations. In many respects this distinction is too general and simplistic, but in this context we may say that without doubt human rights are understood very differently in these three worlds. The attempts to find an answer to the question of human rights are correspondingly different—in theory as well as in practice.

In the rich tradition of Western views on human rights, which were already definitive at the beginning of the ecumenical movement, the rights of the individual, his or her inalienable dignity, and the classical prerogatives were in the forefront: freedom of belief and of conscience, equality of all citizens before the law, legal protection of the citizen from encroachments of the state, the right to property, etc. The emphatic assertion of these rights is understandable in its historical setting. They came into being during the struggles for the rights of citizenship in the face of the accepted political and ecclesiastical institutions; that is, they took shape in the battle which is very deeply anchored in the history of Western society, which however attained its decisive success in the epoch of the establishment of the bourgeoisie during the American and French Revolutions. The classical declarations of human rights, from the American Declaration of Independence (1776) to the Universal Declaration of the United Nations (1948) bear the imprint of this origin: they defend the interests of citizens as free individuals, free producers, free proprietors. Socialist concepts of human rights are distinguished from these individualistic assumptions and their bourgeois elaborations. Especially in the eyes of the Marxist critique, these human rights appeared to be too general and abstract, indeed to be ideological transfigurations—or obfuscations—of real social and economic conditions. In fact, they were criticized for safeguarding no more than the rights of the privileged classes. It must be said that the socialist view in no way disputed the basic intention of protecting human dignity, but agreed that it should be conceived of in more realistic terms and be more effectively actualized through the creation of conditions in society which make it possible for all human beings—above all the heretofore underprivileged—to practice their personal, political, and cultural, but also economic and social rights. This only becomes possible in a socialist society. For this reason it is the socialist perspective on human rights which determines the goal of such a society. The rights of the society then take priority over the interest of private individuals. It was in this sense that in respect to both UN covenants of 1966—The International Covenant on Economic, Social and Cultural Rights and the International Covenant on Civic and Political Rights—the socialist states placed the former in the foreground.

How does the question of human rights take shape for the Third World nations? Here one can hardly speak today of a unified doctrine of human rights. And yet the priorities of these nations have become clearly manifest. Interest centers on the basic exigencies of survival in the face of the famine which threatens so many; on the abolition of colonial structures; on the overcoming of racial discrimination; on the goal of cultural authenticity. In comparison with these collective emergencies the rights of individuals, whose prominence is relatively foreign to the social and cultural traditions of most nations of the Third World, tend to fade. In such a situation human rights mean primarily a demand for life-sustaining conditions for work and nourishment, for an improved balance of life-opportunities between the poor and the rich, for elimination of exploitation within national and international frameworks.

These three divergent concepts of human rights, grasped in terms of their bases, are not mutually exclusive but complementary. In the concrete situation of world politics, however, this interdependence is often not easily recognizable and harmonic but charged with tension and conflict. The different positions ricochet off one another in the world's public forums and in international councils. In this lies a unique opportunity for the ecumenical movement. To be sure, all ecumenical debates will be shaped by the various concepts and interests of the "three worlds," and agreements will thereby be hindered. The passion which has so been persistently kindled on the occasion of human rights discussions within the ecumenical effort illustrates this state of affairs. The faith they hold in common obviously does not redeem Christians from being entangled in the conflicts of their world; rather, it puts them to the test—often a test to the breaking-point—right in the midst of such conflicts. But this is exactly the point: in the midst of these tensions the common faith nevertheless lives. The conflicts do not simply disappear, nor can they be wiped away; yet they may be related to a common basis and a common goal. This is the point from which the various positions may be set in motion. It is at this point that in all our human distress there appear possibilities of ecumenical agreement, which are indeed not without value in the international political context.

The brief history of ecumenical human rights discussions exemplifies this possibility. Its course shows definite turning-points and transformations. The transition from the initial dominance of the bourgeois-liberal doctrine, which had been almost taken for granted, to the adoption in ecumenical consideration and thinking of the socialist critique and of the vital interests of the Third World, might be identified as the most noteworthy. This process did not always evolve in a peaceful way; often it entailed fitful shifts of emphasis. Between Uppsala and Nairobi, some participants from Western nations wondered if the pendulum of ecumenical thought and action had not swung too one-sidedly in the direction of socialist and Third World concepts. In the heat of the battle against racism in the First and Third Worlds, had not the classic concern for religious freedom in the Second World been somewhat neglected?

Ecumenism puts such questions to itself. The dialogue concerning human rights was intensified. And the ecumenical context helped to overcome false pairs of alternatives. The Consultation on Human Rights and Christian Responsibility in St. Pölten, Austria, in October 1974, represented, after years of preparation, the climax of the prevailing process. It brought about quite a bit of tension, but in the end led to a more clearly defined consensus on the stratification and the interdependence of human rights in a divided world.

This is made quite visible in the noteworthy attempt to formulate an ecumenical "Common Ground on Human Rights." It reads:

(a) There is a basic human right to life—inclusive of the entire question of survival, of the threats and violations resulting from unjust economic, social, and political systems, and of the equality of life.

(b) There is a right to enjoy and to maintain cultural identity—which includes issues such as national self-determination, the rights of minorities, etc.

(c) There is a right to participate in the decision-making process within the community—which comprises the entire issue of effective democracy.

(d) There is a right to dissent—which prevents a community or a system from hardening into authoritarian immobility.

(e) There is a right to personal dignity—which implies, for example, the condemnation of all torture and of prolonged confinement without trial.

(f) There is a right freely to choose a faith and a religion—which encompasses the freedom, either alone or in community with others, in public or in private, to proclaim one's faith or one's religion by the means of teaching, practice, worship, and ritual.

In conjunction with this "definition" the consultation spoke of a "common basis." This is justified inasmuch as the ecumenical catalog of human rights, which is not merely static and descriptive but is to be understood as a dynamic correlation of rights, obtained a consensus, which should not be underestimated, regarding these different and yet interrelated human rights. The key phase "common basis" can hardly be done justice, however, in its Christian sense, by such an agreement. It points to a deeper level; it asks the question of the common *theological* ground in the Christian struggle for human rights. That which Christians have in common ecumenically would be too superficially grasped if it were already exhausted in the affirmation of the interdependence of various perspectives. It is only to be gained in common reference to the foundation of faith. It is of the essence to inquire into the theological basis of human rights.

This pressing issue was hardly posed by the consultation at St. Pölten, as Ludwig Raiser rightly noted in the article cited at the beginning of the essay. Ecumenical theologians should prick up their ears when an involved lawyer remarks in response to consultation that it will "demand deepened theological reflection in order to work out the specifically Christian contribution to the further development of the human rights issue."[1]

---

[1] *Evangelische Kommentare*, 1975, p. 201.

II. Towards a Theological Basis for Human Rights

One attempt to take on this assignment is represented by the study of the department of theology of the World Alliance of Reformed Churches, certain documents and findings of which are being published in this book. This program of study originated with the recommendation of the General Assembly of the WARC in Nairobi (1970). "Theological Basis of Human Rights and the Theology of Liberation" was one of three problem areas with which the theological department was to deal during the preparatory period of 1970-77.

The first general inquiry into opinions among the member churches, which I undertook as chairman of this department along with Richmond Smith as secretary, demonstrated that the human rights program had already been granted unequivocal priority. This was not altogether surprising. In addition to the general ecumenical reasons I have indicated for the present intensity of human rights issues, there is a special reason in the case of the Reformed churches: Reformed theology has historically dedicated itself with unique fervor to questions of responsible formation of the social realm, of political responsibility, and of the rights of citizens in Christian perspective. The deficit of interest, indeed the "deep-seated aversions to the modern human rights movement," discerned by H. E. Tödt in German Lutheranism,[2] can hardly be said of Reformed theology. Especially in Anglo-Saxon Presbyterianism, human rights considerations and initiatives have played a significant social and economic role. Indeed, in this realm one family of Reformed churches has had enduring and authentic commitments.

The formulation of the theme deserves attention on two points. First, according to the statement of its General Assembly in 1970 the WARC was not interested in a general study of human rights but rather in its *theological basis*. From the beginning the goal was decidedly not to produce a declaration which might be duplicated in the declarations of other ecumenical or secular councils. The intent was to inquire into the specifically Christian perspective for our human rights effort, its theological foundation and motivation. This was not intended to establish distance from other movements and fellow human beings and thus to silhouette itself righteously over against them, but to encourage our churches to committed—which means theologically grounded—involvement. Even from the practical

---

[2] "Human Rights as the Frame of Reference for Church Action," in *epd Documentation* 5/75, p. 110.

viewpoint, this is not without significance. We must surely not forget that theological lack of clarity can considerably weaken the credibility and effectuality of Christian witness and service.

Second, the title of the study unmistakably binds the question of human rights to the question of liberation. This connection counteracts from the outset the possible misunderstanding of human rights as a set of static values which ideologically glorify the transmitted status quo, as though they were "luxury articles" for the privileged. The traditionally dominant foundation of human rights in natural law, with its static character, has occasionally given rise to such a suspicion, especially in the eyes of the underprivileged. The allusion to liberation places human rights in the dynamic context of the search for greater justice. This comes closer not only to the situation of the oppressed and the disenfranchised, but also to the dynamics of the biblical message: the world of human beings is interpreted and transformed not according to generalized natural laws, but according to the history of liberation of Jesus Christ, thus in the perspective of the kingdom of God and its justice.

As far as the factual development of the study is concerned, the following background information may be helpful for understanding the documents involved. The theological department of the WARC commissioned Jürgen Moltmann to write a "starter" paper for the member churches.[3] Moltmann defined the position of the human rights issue within the context of the "political worship" of our churches: *"The political and social directions of the churches gain their universal significance* only in their relationship to human rights. With regard to human rights, the church necessarily becomes the 'church for others' or the 'church for the world.'"* The paper offered an overview of the sources and development of the idea of human rights, as well as a suggestion for the process of the study, in the form of the following three steps:

1. Christian theology is theology of liberation, for it understands Christ in the comprehensive sense as liberator.
2. The theology of liberation is the theology of man, for every man is defined by his similitude to God.
3. The theology of liberation is the theology of the future, for the kingdom of the Son of Man is the human future of man.

---

[3] Chapter 2 below; first published in *The Experiment Hope*, Philadelphia: Fortress Press, 1975.

The outline for the study echoed positively among the member churches. Many churches of the Reformed, Calvinist, and Congregational family commissioned their own theological committees, faculties, or even individuals to formulate position papers. These contributions were directed to the theological department in Geneva. The spectrum of the voices was extraordinarily broad. It extended from Taiwan and Korea to Brazil, from South Africa to Northern Ireland, from East Germany to the United States. There were comprehensive lists of theses, as well as glosses and spontaneous reactions. It was no easy task to incorporate the variegated material and to coordinate it according to different emphases. The fact that both the North American Area Committee and the European Area Commission were fully engaged in the work, and that they prepared and presented their positions on the basis of repeated consultations, became very significant for the work of the WARC. The North Americans stressed the correlation of human rights and liberation, supporting themselves with an entire series of preparatory papers by members and guests (chapters 6–10 below). The work of the European commission, which in addition to reports from several member churches in the West and the East, had in particular the studies of Daniel Vidal of Spain (see chapter 4) and Hannelore Erhart-Jahr (East Germany) at its disposal, dealt with the plurality of viewpoints in contemporary Europe and the readiness to hear the voices of different cultural realms. Summarizing theses which arose from the work of both commissions are printed in this book (chapters 3 and 5). The preliminary conclusion and, indeed, the high point of the study process is represented by the theological consultation in London, February 1976, summoned by the theological department of the WARC. It was a relatively small group of theologians, pastors and laypersons, especially fitted to carry out this task due to its perspicuity and inclusiveness: some twenty persons from no fewer than fourteen nations. Member churches from all continents were represented. This provided the requisite multiplicity of viewpoints and facilitated their hearing of the concerns of fellow Christians more strongly informed by other conditions: a fundamental requirement for a truly ecumenical agreement concerning human rights. The participation of the director of the WCC Commission of the Churches on International Affairs, Leopoldo Niilus, was a further advantage: the connection with the work of the WCC in this realm was thereby established.

The concluding study by Jürgen Moltmann (chapter 11) stood at the focal point of the consultation. Thus the initiator of the task was also entrusted with its summary. In this way the continuity of the ecumenical process of learning, on the one hand, and the growth of understanding from the "starter" to the closing study on the other, were illuminated. I perceive three points which demonstrate a certain progress: (1) The ecumenical dimension of the problematic of human rights receives more careful attention in the course of the study; non-European aspects are more strongly incorporated; (2) in the theological approach the fundamental idea of the grounding of human rights in "God's right to, i.e. his claim upon, human beings" is granted central importance; and thus (3) though the motif of "theology of liberation" recedes somewhat as an explicit theme, it continues to operate in the manner in which the rights of humanity and the equivalent tasks of the churches are understood.

The London consultation gratefully appropriated the Moltmann study, inquired of it further, and encouraged the author to follow through in the light of the ensuing discussions. In addition, the participants worked out in an intensive exchange a two-part recommendation of "Theological Guidelines" and "Some Practical Implications" (chapter 12 below). With this the study drew to a temporary end.

The documents speak for themselves. If, however, in conclusion, I were to lift up three points which seem to me especially noteworthy in this ecumenical deliberation on human rights, I would mention the following three aspects.

1. *The basis of fundamental human rights is God's right to—that is, claim on—the human being.* In its attempt to clarify unequivocally the theological ground of the Christian human rights effort, the study does not operate within the traditional context of natural law, of the anthropological (idealistic) or the historical (materialistic) explanation. It does not understand human rights as timeless components of either the nature of the human being, nor as acquisitions of the historical, revolutionary self-salvation of the human race, but rather understands them in terms of the central theme of the gospel: that of the covenant of the faithful God to God's people and to creation. The right to be a person is anchored in God's right to us as human beings, not in an abstract and arbitrary sense, but in the way in which this claim was given concrete and binding articulation in the biblical history of salvation and liberation.

Moltmann interpreted the basic intention and the practical consequences of this approach "from above" (as it is misleadingly called) in the following words:

21

We wanted in this way to underscore the *theological* contribution of Christian theology. This is intended to be neither totalitarianism nor indoctrination. This approach does however have the advantage of giving universal regard to—and of demanding the regard of—the dignity and rightful claim of every person. On the other hand, any approach "from below," from the basis of experience, remains of necessity limited and selective, because our experience is limited and because the universality of what is human can only be gleaned through extrapolation of what one holds it to be. The theological method being applied here transmits today the witness of biblical history, so that a common history arises, one having as content divine liberation, the covenant with the liberating God, and the rights and stipulations of this freedom.[4]

2. *Emphasis on the holistic and interdependent character of human rights.* Anchored in God's claim on the whole person, the study takes the stance of an encompassing view of human rights. This is not only to be understood in the sense of the ecumenical complementarity of the differing perspectives of all three worlds; this aspect had already been convincingly elaborated in St. Pölten and was then incorporated into the thought-processes of the London consultation. These documents contradict any understanding of "individual" and "social" rights as "alternatives," whereby it is stressed that—in view of the temptations and dangers of the particular society—the churches should protectively and productively set appropriate priorities. Thus, in a bourgeois-capitalistic society, the often undervalued social and economic rights need repeatedly to be reaffirmed, whereas in a Marxist-socialist society it is necessary to intervene in the name of the usually underdeveloped rights to the freedom of conscience and of faith worthy of a human being.

In London supplementary emphases were added. Thus the consultation presented the "ecumenical dimension" not only in an historical and temporal sense: the rights of contemporaries should not remain the only framework for responsible theory and praxis of human rights. Rights of future generations are also to be taken into account. Any *"après-nous-le-deluge"* attitude on the part of individuals and collectivities endangers the chances for the survival of our descendants, offends in this way against the "claim of God on human beings," and perverts the claims of humanity. This viewpoint proceeds today from empirical evidence regarding human intercourse with nature, and addresses a further accent of the study: it is our task to protect the wholeness and interdependence of human rights in the

4 *Evangelische Kommentare,* 1976, 5, p. 281.

context of the creation as well. God's claim on human beings does not occur in isolation but is linked to God's claim on other creatures, whereby the rights of these creatures are set in relationship to ours. According to this understanding of human rights, we must strive for ecological as well as for economic justice.

3. *Christian perspectives on human rights.* The consultation and certain of the documents from the study process (such as Daniel Vidal's contribution) were concerned to articulate specifically Christian motifs and insights. This is not limited to the oft-mentioned starting point of God's claim on human beings. That which is specifically Christian was brought into focus both in the whole outlook and in its execution. Thus the gospel's central motifs of reconciliation and of the free grace of God were unmistakably emphasized. This happened not as a sort of exercise of theological duty; rather, the conviction had been reached that it is indeed in view of the inevitable and almost insoluble conflicts into which we are hurtled by a commitment to human rights—in the face of their large-scale violations—that this view can contribute to liberation; for as the "Theological Guidelines" state, it "prevents us from despairing in situations of overwhelming and frustrating set-backs. At the same time it prevents our involvement in the struggle for human rights from becoming a self-righteous justification by works, rather than a thoroughgoing repentance and self-giving investment in justice and freedom as a response to our having been justified by God's grace alone." Understood in this sense, the emphasis on a "Christian perspective on human rights" does not imply a recommendation for a special "Christian show," for a solitary and exclusive path in the realm of human rights, and it is certainly not at all an argument for the defense of "Christian privileges." On the contrary. That which is "distinctively Christian" does not establish privileges, but compels—in the sense of Jesus—unconditional openness and commitment to others. A truly *Christian* perspective implies rights for Christians only in the context of *human* rights: "fellow human" rights.

This dialectic of the specifically Christian *and* of the inclusively human belongs, if I understand it correctly, to the most essential of the insights and characteristics of the London consultation and its documents. Moltmann is in agreement when he formulates the following lines in retrospect:

It is when Christianity is fulfilling its uniquely "Christian tasks" that it serves the humanness of all human beings. Conversely, it fulfils its uniquely "Christian tasks" inasmuch as it serves the humanness of all human beings.

23

"By proclaiming God's justifying grace, it proclaims the dignity of human beings. By practicing the right of grace, it practices basic human rights." Community with Jesus, the "Son of Man," leads it into suffering with the oppression of human beings, into resistance against tyranny and the sustaining prayer for the coming of God. Thus Christianity is not only externally and accidentally concerned with human rights, but internally, essentially, and with the whole of its existence.[5]

To incite and to encourage our member churches, our fellow Christians, and ourselves to remember these correlations, to examine and to develop further the insights gained—this is the intention and the hope of our efforts toward a theological basis for human rights.

[5] *Ibid.*, p. 282.

2. The Original Study Paper: A Theological Basis of Human Rights and of the Liberation of Human Beings

JÜRGEN MOLTMANN

I. The Current Situation

From its inception the ecumenical movement has been conscious of its connection with political movements for the international recognition of human rights. "We observe with pleasure the development of an international awareness of responsibility for the respect of human rights" (First General Assembly of the Lutheran World Federation, Lund, 1947). Session IV, Art. 17–22, of the Fourth General Assembly of the World Council of Churches in Uppsala, expressly acknowledged

> that the development of social justice in all human relationships presupposes that human dignity is recognized and protected and that the full equality of men of all races and nations as well as of the adherents of all religions and ideologies will become the common goal of the community of nations (Art. 17).

The Fifth General Assembly of the LWF in Evian, France (1970) took the following stand: "The churches should be summoned to search for ways, means, and opportunities of enabling their members to study the Universal Declaration of Human Rights and to undertake the application of this declaration in the national life of their member churches." Articles 1, 5, 9, 10, 18, 19, and 26 were explicitly cited. It

Jürgen Moltmann is professor of systematic theology at the University of Tübingen and a special consultant to the department of theology of the WARC in pursuing this study. This position-paper, written in 1971, has served as the "starter" for our entire project. The translation from the German was made by M. Douglas Meeks, associate professor of theology and ethics, Eden Theological Seminary, St. Louis.

is therefore time to think through in a fundamental way the theological basis of human rights, so that this summons does not remain a declaration to which we are not really bound.

The political and social directions of the churches gain their universal significance only in their relationship to human rights. With regard to human rights, the church necessarily becomes the "church for others" or the "church for the world." The decision of the WCC in Arnoldshain, September, 1970, arising out of this understanding of the church, to give public and financial support to the anti-racism program has its basis in a theology of human rights. It aroused resistance and confusion precisely because many member churches have neglected to study human rights. In opposition to the resolutions we have mentioned, they have considered these concerns alien to their task as the church. They did not recognize, nor did they want to recognize, the Christian character of the declarations of human rights.

What theological relevance do declarations of human rights have for the political and social practice of Christianity in the world? What relevance does the political and social existence of the church have for the spreading and the realization of human rights?

II. The History of the Declaration of Human Rights

Cultural anthropology has pointed out that the perception and acknowledgement of *man* is a rather recent phenomenon. There were cultures in which the term *man* was reserved exclusively for the members of one's own tribe; strangers were not viewed as men. In its primitive form this ethnocentrism has its roots in the fact that early languages knew only few abstract concepts. In these languages there are palms, cedars, and oaks but not yet the inclusive concept *tree*. Thus there are fellow tribesmen and strangers but as yet no word for common humanity. Psychology has demonstrated that the present-day refusal to recognize others as men happens intentionally. War propaganda notoriously makes enemies subhuman: Jews, Russians, Japs, gooks, niggers, communists, miserable dogs, and so on. They are the barbarians who are known only as enemies and may live only as slaves. Thus men identify humanity with the positives they possess—race, caste, class, religion, and the like—and project the inhuman, which they want to repress in themselves, onto the stranger who is different. Self-assertion and declassification of the other, self-justification and hatred of the strangers, are nourished by the demonic compulsion of man to self-affirmation.

26

The concept of *humanitas*, which is common to Greeks and barbarians, emerges in our cultural sphere in the philosophy of the Sophists and the Stoics. All men are equals on the basis of their common human nature. Their distinctions are determined merely externally and historically. The common human nature is self-evident by virtue of the inborn ideal of reason which is common to all. Cicero placed over against the ancient Roman idea of *homo romanus* the higher ideal of *homo humanus*. The corresponding antithesis is therefore no longer Roman or barbarian, free man or slave, but human and inhuman among Romans and barbarians, among free men or slaves.

Where, in other cultural spheres, are there comparable developments of the concepts of humanity?

Another concept of humanity parallel to this emerged from the biblical traditions. Adam was not the first Jew but the first man. If God the Creator fashioned man in his image on earth, then the inner dignity, freedom, and responsibility of man extends impartially beyond every human community and state organization. It is not a king, as in the ideology of the pharaohs, but man, who is the image of God on earth. If God acts as the liberator of man in an inhuman history, then the goal of Israel as well as of Christianity is the new, just humanity of God. The historical monotheism of the Old Testament leads logically to the notion of one humanity. Before God, all individual destinies and national histories merge into a single and common world history. The late Israelite expectation of the coming kingdom of the Son of man (Daniel 7), which will overcome the "beastly kingdoms of the world," and the Christian proclamation of Jesus as the Son of man and the new man display a theological and future-oriented concept of humanity. Here it is not a question of a common human nature knitting together different men. Rather their common definition in terms of the similitude of God and their common future in the coming kingdom of God bind them together in such a way that their historical differences are to be overcome. "Every valley shall be lifted up, and every mountain and hill be made low"; so that "all flesh together" can see the glory of the Lord (Isa. 40:4, 5).

Only in the sixteenth century do human rights emerge as instruments in the political struggle for the legal security of the individual against the coercion of the state. Their development is not yet finished.

The Christianization of the European states transformed the relationship of man to the state in a twofold manner. (1) If man is God's image, he is a responsible person and bearer of the rights and duties of freedom (Boethius: *rationalis naturae individua substantia*). Man does not exist for the sake of the state, but the state for the sake of man. (2) The state is therefore no longer "God on earth," but has to respect and guard the dignity of man. With this, human rights become the basic rights of state constitutions. Basic rights are the standards by which civil rights and state power must be criticized and judged. That state power is not taken for granted, but must be justified, is a result of the Christianization of these states.

Yet the religious and theoretical right of human freedom (in faith and before God) and factual social and political unfreedom remained intertwined throughout the Middle Ages. Basically only the nobles secured privileges for themselves by means of contracts with monarchs (e.g., the *Magna Charta Liberatum*, 1215). They brought into our history, however, the notion of the state contract, through which political power became limited and controllable. On this ground English Puritanism developed the *Rights of Parliament* in the *Petition of Rights* (1628) and the *Bill of Rights* (1689). The protective aspect of human rights was developed at this time: guarantee against illegal incarceration, guarantee of religious freedom, and so on. Only with the American *Declaration of the Rights of Virginia* (1776) was that government or state contract finally ruled legal by constitution. The constitution or covenant understands human rights "as the basis and foundation of government." "All men are by nature equally free and independent, and have certain inherent rights. . . ." These rights are seen as self-evident axioms of every human policy. Yet in this declaration of the foundations of the constitution a specific declaration of intention is missing with regard to the concrete distinctions between rights and property among whites and slaves, among rich and poor.

In the first article of the French Constitution of 1791 such an intention is more concretely stressed. "Men are born free and equal in rights and remain so. Social differences can be grounded only on the common needs." The *droit de l'homme* is translated into the *droit du citoyen*. In the nineteenth century the middle class, which had borne the human rights movement, more and more renounced the intention of emancipation of man from rule and inequality and increasingly stressed the protective side of the state for the guaranteeing of stability to human rights and individual freedoms.

Out of the Russian Revolution arose a constitution of the exploited against the exploiters. Article three of the Constitution of the Russian Socialist Federated Congress of Republics (1918) includes these words: "in struggle to destroy every exploitation of man by

28

man, every class division of society, unmercifully to crush the exploiters. . . ." Also the Constitution of the Union of Soviet Socialist Republics (1936) calls rights which merely preserve the state no protection against state encroachments. The state constitution is here essentially severed from the tradition of middle-class human rights.

The Fascist terror in Europe led in the West to the Atlantic Charter in 1941, and after the war to the establishment of the United Nations (San Francisco, 1945), whose Universal Declaration of Human Rights (1948) is recognized up to the present as the internationally binding statement of human rights. Because of the experiences of tyranny, the protective side of the state *vis-à-vis* the human rights allegedly under its care is obviated. It represents social demands which go beyond the middle-class limitation to individual freedoms. Finally, the future character of human rights is emphasized. After the preamble "the General Assembly proclaims the Universal Declaration of Rights which is before us as the common ideal to be attained by all peoples and nations. . . ." It contains therefore not only a declaration of the basis but also a declaration of intent. But how we are to get from this ideal to its practical realization remains unexplained because the United Nations lacks the power for realization. Since then, however, human rights have won an international character and are not openly disputed by any nation.

III. Theological Problems of Human Rights

Human rights have issued out of the process of the Christianization of societies and states. The vital dignity of the human person as an object of concern has taken shape in legal and political institutions. The actual liberation and the experienced freedom of man have already been realized in laws and institutions of freedom. The process of Christianization exists between church life specifically and political life in general. Whether they work in evolutionary or revolutionary ways, the present struggles for a better humanity and a more radical liberation must find their bearings in relation to these processes. Otherwise they are in the air and without relationship to anything. The revolution of freedom also knows the tradition of freedom and has to take it up into itself.

The well-known declarations of human rights we have mentioned, however, are effective only insofar as there are men who are prepared to take upon themselves the rights and duties of men and stand up for the oppressed for the sake of humanity. The rights of freedom are effective only insofar as there are free men who intercede for the liberation of enslaved men. The question is whether and to what extent present-day living Christianity actualizes a reality for humanity and freedom which fills these human rights with social and political life.

Two principal questions can be posed to the Universal Declaration of Human Rights:

(1) *What functions can this declaration serve?* It can be understood as a *universal fundament* of various national constitutions. The several civil rights are then derived from the basic rights of man and must be judged by them. But in the case of conflict, who or what takes precedence: human rights as related to fundamental rights or national security?

It can be understood, in the second place, as a *common ideal* of the nations. Then the fundamental intention of the declaration of human rights is a society of humanity on earth in which the egoism of national foreign policy is eliminated and replaced by a mutual world domestic policy. But in the case of conflict, who or what takes precedence: the desired society of humanity or the interest of one's own nation?

Whether understood as universal fundament or as universal ideal of separate nations, the weaknesses of human rights exist in the fact that there are too few powers for realizing them over against injustice and oppression. They can very easily be misused as the intellectual facade of evil. Often, fundamental declarations have a mere decorative character and in actuality serve the concealment of the opposite. How much unfreedom is there in the "free world?" How much unbrotherliness is there in the "socialist world?" Ideals, if one takes them seriously, can change reality. But they can also become the mere justification of good intentions, without a corresponding will for realization. It is really a matter then of clarifying the relationship of the theory of human rights to practice in order to exclude misuse. But the practical fulfilment of human rights is humanity for the oppressed. The practical realization of freedom is the liberation of the enslaved. The practical function of this Universal Declaration of Human Rights therefore can only be revolutionary.

(2) *In what respect should the Declaration of Human Rights be supplemented if it is to have, not an idealistic, but a revolutionary significance?* The ideal rights of man can certainly be extended. For example, the present definitions of the right to the freedom of religion are deficient. In my opinion, however, it would be more

important to extend human rights with reference to social obligations. For me, the decisive issue is the transformation of rights which secure the freedom of individuals into obligations to liberate those whose rights are withheld by others. If the Universal Declaration of Human Rights is not to be only an ideal suspended above an inhuman world, but desires the realization of these rights, then rights must be articulated in terms of their realization. Up to the present time there is nothing expressed in the Universal Declaration about suffering within the world which is necessarily entailed in the struggle for liberation.

What theological links between the Christian faith and the tradition of human rights are capable of bearing weight and are fruitful?

These connecting concepts emerge historically in the process of humanization and Christianization of the world and have a historically shaped and delineated form. They stand between concrete Christian practice and universal humanity as political and legal forms of life.

The theological tradition has perennially connected Christian practice and universal humanity by means of a Christian doctrine of natural law and a Christian doctrine of creation. This connection is only a theoretical one. The existing right of man is explained as a reflection of the right of God. By this means it is both recognized and maintained. A Christian doctrine of natural law really has nothing to add to the natural law. Rather, in every case it has to free it from misuse.

For this study I would like to propose another way. In order to sketch that theory which grounds this event of liberation and makes it universally binding and which does this by defining man in terms of the freedom of his similitude to God, should we not begin from the concrete practice of the liberation of the unfree man through faith, love, and hope? Should we not begin with the practice of liberation in order then to outline that theory which combines this historical event with hope in the human kingdom of the new man and makes it accessible for every human being?

In the Old Testament, theological thought begins with Yahweh's liberation-history with Israel in the Exodus and only afterward, and on this basis, comes to the confession that this God of liberation is the Creator of all things and the Redeemer of all people. In the New Testament, too, theological thought begins with the confession of Christ as the liberator and only then, and on this basis, comes to the doctrine of creation and to eschatology.

Translating this into a theology of human rights would likewise mean beginning with the concrete theology of liberation and on this basis presenting the universal meaning of this freedom as universal human right and the common future of this freedom as new humanity.

I think that only with this concrete starting point in the theology of liberation can universal theories and declarations about the freedom of man be protected from their misuse.

Thus I conceive the theological process of such a grounding in three steps:

(1) *Christian theology is theology of liberation, for it understands Christ in the comprehensive sense as liberator.*

(2) *The theology of liberation is the theology of man, for every man is defined by his similitude to God.*

(3) *The theology of liberation is the theology of the future, for the kingdom of the Son of man is the human future of man.*

Questions posed to step 1:

How does the Bible look if we read it with the eyes of the poor, the hungry, the outcasts, and the oppressed? Do we not assume a false standpoint over against the Bible when we read it as a book of religion or as a book of law or as a book of dogmatic ideologies, while failing to stand in solidarity with the oppressed?

The sick, the possessed, the leprous, the humiliated, and the godless experienced Jesus as a concrete liberator from their concrete misery and they believed in this liberation. From what is Christianity seeking to liberate men in the discipleship of Jesus, in its proclamation, its community, and its deeds? Do we understand faith as a concrete event of liberation or do we believe only in a freedom which does not really exist? Do we understand Jesus, in the comprehensive sense, as liberator from every unfreedom and inhumanity, or do we consider him only a religious liberator?

Jesus is experienced as liberator by those who are bound, by the oppressed and the guilt-laden; and their community with him is concrete freedom from their chains, their oppressions, and their guilt. But he was crucified by the powers and the principalities of the world according to their law. If they do not persecute Christianity today, they nevertheless would like to take the dangerous power of liberation away from it. How then is Christ conceived? As Lord of heaven, a new lawgiver, an unpolitical religious founder, or a guardian of order?

On which side does the church stand in one's own country? Has it become the political religion of the powerful in order to receive their goodwill and money? In each of our several countries, where and how does liberation for the oppressed proceed from ecclesiastical institutions and Christian actions?

Questions posed to step 2:

If a theology of liberation is a theology of man, because every man is defined by the image of God, then church and Christian practice can be realized not only in church and Christian circles, but must make the questions of man its own question. Yet how can the Christian caste-spirit and the mistrust of others be overcome?

For whom is the question of man the most important? For the inhuman, the dehumanized. Consequently, a church which makes the question of man its own question cannot simply "exist for all men"; it must exist for those robbed of human rights and freedoms. How can the church become the community of the poor and the oppressed and dissolve its ties with others who make them poor and oppress them?

What means can Christianity use for the liberation of man to freedom? Missionary means or also humanitarian measures? When is the use of revolutionary force necessary for the liberation of the oppressed? Can it be that, on the basis of existing declarations of human rights in particular countries, institutionalized tyranny is manifested? For example: (a) politically, through the rule of military cliques; (b) radically, through the predominance of a white minority; (c) socially, through the predominance of an exploiting class?

If an obvious tyranny has no right to power, is revolutionary power then justified?

Who is justified in and obligated to resistance? Is there a right of the people to revolution, as earlier in the church there was a right of the congregation to reformation?

In such situations can the political responsibility of individual Christians be distinguished from the commission of the church?

Questions posed to step 3:

Which ideal of the future is depicted in the Universal Declaration of Human Rights? Can it be combined with the hope in the "human kingdom of the Son of man," which, according to Daniel 7, is to cut off the kingdoms of the world?

To what degree does the Christian hope in the kingdom of God support, and to what extent does it criticize, the hope in the coming society of humanity, which is expressed in human rights?

How can there develop out of the ideal of human rights a concrete utopia which relates the intended human future of man to the specific political, social, and racial injustice of the present in order to overcome opposition and resistance? By whom is this future of man represented today? By the public? How can the conscience of the world public be sharpened? By Christianity? How can the *oekumene* speak representatively for Christians who in certain countries cannot speak publicly? Does this damage the difficult position of those Christians or does it assist the struggle for liberation? Does the ecumenical bond of the churches give individual churches and Christians more independence over against the coercion of their own nation and social order? Does the struggle for the realization of human rights not presuppose an inner break in the national egoism and the class intellect or the racial mind-set? If Christians find their identity in the crucified Christ, then what relevance can national, cultural, and economic identity still have for them?

3. A European Response

REMKO MOOI

I. Starting Points

1. The Bible does not speak of rights and liberties, which are due to mankind by nature, but of a justice and a liberation, which are given to men and women by God.

2. Therefore the church must make its starting point in biblical suppositions, not in natural law.

3. The liberation granted by God and witnessed to by the church is directed not only to individuals, but also to the nations and to the whole world.

4. Therefore the attitude of the Christian to all people shall be that of solidarity. Such solidarity proceeds directly from the position in which God has placed human beings and from the justice which he has granted the world.

5. Both creation and the fact that God permitted the fall of humanity indicate how much God created the world for freedom and how much he wants to be served in freedom.

6. It is exactly for that purpose that Jesus Christ has redeemed the world which was handed over to sin and guilt.

7. Therefore Christians regard freedom of thought, conscience, and religion as one of the most important liberties (Universal Declaration of Human Rights, Art. XVIII). God who gives freedom can only be met in freedom.

8. The universality of the biblical conception of creation implies that the church looks at men and women principally as human beings, notwithstanding their origin, race, or religion. Since in the past the church has not been completely faithful to this biblical starting point,

Remko Mooi is assistant general secretary of the Netherlands Reformed Church, The Hague. The European Theological Commission of WARC was chaired from 1967 to 1973 by J. K. S. Reid, professor emeritus of systematic theology, University of Aberdeen; and since 1973 by G. E. Meuleman, professor of philosophy of religion, Free University of Amsterdam.

it has to be specifically stated that it often did not understand its own message.

II. Content

1. Christian theology is theology of liberation, for it looks to Jesus Christ as liberator in an all-inclusive sense.

2. When Jesus Christ is understood in this way as liberator and the essence of his work is seen in this, then liberation has to be considered as liberation from sin and guilt and in close connection with forgiveness and redemption.

3. The doctrine of Jesus Christ as the liberator lays a necessary emphasis on the inner connection between his work and the social situation of life, in which men and women are living. Being human is not being to oneself, but being human in the context of society.

4. The theology of liberation includes an essential anthropological dimension, for every human being is destined to be the image of God.

5. Therefore liberation is to be characterized as the coming of men and women to their fulfilment; and this can be expressed by the all-inclusive idea *freedom,* which God intends for his creation.

6. The theology of liberation is the theology of the future, for the kingdom of the Son of man is the human future of humanity.

7. Therefore the Christian faith is essentially a firm confidence in the eventual completion of the work of the God who acts. All work that serves liberation takes place in the context of the coming kingdom and receives from it its sense and meaning.

III. Function

1. Human rights become effective wholly through the action of men and women, who are prepared to bring these rights into practice. Living Christianity has to function in the world as a source of humanity and freedom. There is no Christian understanding of human rights without a closely connected praxis.

2. This does not mean that Christian liberty is only given where it can be realized in the context of political power. It is important to stress that the freedom which is received from Christ is not to be seen apart from a living concern which is directed to the care of the victims of oppression and suffering and the removal of the basic causes.

3. For the Christian there is no faith without action, no action without faith.

4. Human rights provide a common basis for national and international legislation. As such they function as basic rights.

5. Human rights function as a common ideal for the nations. These rights direct the attention of all nations and all governments to the ideal of one community of human beings on earth in which the policies of different societies would not be in conflict.

6. The Christian faith is a source of inspiration and vocation for all who can understand the gospel. The realization, however, of a society without oppression and domination is inconceivable apart from the intensive cooperation of men and women of different thinking, feeling, and believing. Belief should have such conviction as brings others to the same conviction.

7. From a philosophical anthropological perspective the right understanding of each individual of his or her humanity is possible only in the light of the humanity of the other, the fellow-creature.

8. Care must be especially taken that human rights not be abused to disguise deeds which are essentially directed to the oppression of individuals or groups.

9. It is possible that the pursuit of human rights will have a revolutionary aspect.

IV. Critical Questions

1. Consideration should be given to enlarging the understanding of human rights with a clearer description of freedom of thought, conscience, and religion (Universal Declaration of Human Rights, Art. XVIII).

2. Also of great importance is an explicit mention of the social duties of being human, especially with regard to the oppressed.

3. For the realization of human rights account must be taken not only of violence in the common sense of the word, but also of structural violence as the cause of the difference between the potential and the actual in human self-realization as far as the structures of society are concerned. Therefore the structures of society, including the church-state relationship, have to be analyzed at all levels—local, national, and international.

4. Violence should not be equated with radicalism and revolution, nor nonviolence with gradualism and reform, nor vice versa. The question is: how can humanity be served, under the oppressing force of a ruling power, or under the involving force of a revolutionary movement?

* * * * *

It is proposed that further consideration be given to a possible section on historical considerations.

1. In the course of history various conceptions of human rights have emerged and been formulated.

2. The question can be raised whether this is to be considered as a process of Christianizing, as some are inclined to assume. Other philosophical conceptions such as Stoic philosophy and neo-Platonism have been of considerable influence.

3. In their conception of human rights Christians have always been children of their time. Human rights have not been applied equally to all races and to all social classes.

4. In the nineteenth century the main accent of interest shifted from the emancipation of men and women from servitude and inequality to the protective function of the state. The state was looked on as the guarantor of these rights. In this context we find the criticism of Marxism of the middle-class formulation of basic human rights.

5. The historical foundation of basic rights has no sufficient protection against arbitrary and uncritical alterations. Therefore the Christian has to rely on the concrete praxis of the liberation of the unfree person by Jesus Christ.

4. Examining the European Commission's Theses

DANIEL VIDAL

My task in this paper is to explore in greater depth the theses adopted by the European theological commission (pp. 35–38) in response to Professor Moltmann's essay (pp. 25–34). I am perfectly aware of my limitations—some personal, some environmental, and some due to Barthian or other influences which color my theological work. I would add that my thinking has been profoundly stimulated by the study of the document of the Vaudois churches of Latin America (which is not surprising if we realize, *mutatis mutandis*, the similarity of the situations) and also by the document of the theological commission of the Remonstrant Brotherhood in Holland.

It seems to me that we ought to take a theological stance that is realistic enough to oblige us to ask ourselves certain basic questions about the Universal Declaration of Human Rights of the United Nations and about our own prejudices as Western Christians. I hasten to say that in my opinion we can neither try to renounce our Western position nor take it too seriously. But at the same time we ought to realize that we greatly risk falling into a basic contradiction when we ascribe to those who are not at first hand Western the same presuppositions we received through our history. The Declaration of the United Nations is an outstanding example of that.

I also intend to remain within my tradition when I try to think about the theological basis of human rights. That is, by theological basis I mean confrontation with the tenets of the Christian faith and not at all a basis which can be found in any theology or religion whatsoever. Furthermore, I am striving to think within "the Reformed faith," although I am theoretically aware of my Roman Catholic tradition from the very fact of my environment and its history.

Rights—human rights, for in a certain sense one could also speak of the rights of dogs or of the rights of nature—have a fundamental

Daniel Vidal is dean of the Evangelical Seminary, Madrid, and president of the Spanish Evangelical Church. The translation of this paper from the original French was made by Olive P. Eggers, Webster Groves High School, St. Louis.

presupposition: freedom. Of the thirty articles of the UN Declaration, fourteen mention specifically and in different contexts freedom in the sense of "freedom of . . ."; and practically all mention it either by synonyms (in the specific sense of the basic philosophy of the Declaration, "equality" or "dignity") or by paraphrases. It is therefore necessary to find a theological meaning for the basic presupposition of the Declaration, that is, of freedom itself, if one wants to succeed in finding such for the manifestations of freedom in rights. We will begin with some critical remarks about this very important document, and continue with a more specifically theological approach.

I. The UN Declaration: Some Critical Remarks

The thirty articles of the UN Declaration seem to be conditioned by the first article. Indeed, whether they be juridical questions or questions related to education, everything is related to freedom, to equality, to dignity, and to rights mentioned in the first article. Moreover, the right to private property, expressly mentioned in Article 17, is a consequence of the equality which is taken for granted in Article 1 and developed in the articles referring to education "for freedom" (26 and 27) and in the article which establishes the "right to work" (23). The first article develops a theme which is well known in European thinking, but which is misleading if one refers to history or biology, and even more so if one refers to theology. It is quite simply utopian to say that all men are born free and with the same dignity and the same rights. That perhaps expresses a desire, but it does not express either an historical or a scientific reality. But if one adds that they have been given the ability to reason and a conscience (by whom?), that is to go back to the utterly obsolete category of man as a thinking animal who has been given a natural moral—so-called Christian—conscience. That permits the expression of the good, ideal desire for a brotherly attitude. On the one hand, one is still at the level of the French Revolution, with its "liberty, equality, fraternity," and on the other hand at the level of rationalist theory, which assures us that natural liberty, equality, and fraternity progress toward perfection through education.

Philosophically, we have the right to ask ourselves, first of all, if freedom is thereby confused with equality, whether if one succeeded in proving that the latter no longer exists, the former in its turn would disappear. Perhaps we ought also to ask ourselves if freedom—and only freedom, for it is clear that equality is conceivable only juridically and not existentially—is a condition of the human being without reference to decision as an act which creates freedom, as existentialist criticism would say. It goes without saying that Marxist criticism would be still more radical. But without going that far, and in accordance with Ortega y Gasset's idea of man, we can cast doubt on that freedom which would be intrinsic to every human being by the fact that he or she is human (it would still be necessary to agree on what "human" means). If Ortega y Gasset is right, my environment is constitutive of my awareness of myself and by definition environments are different from historical, biological, and cultural points of view. It is difficult, if not impossible, to think of an equal freedom in an unequal context and of equality in an unequal possibility of freedom.

But our goal is not to give a philosophical criticism (to do so one would have to deal with many other elements, such as symbols and language) but to ask ourselves some theological questions. Already there appears a first purely theological question. Is it possible, in the context of the Christian faith, to speak of human rights, or must one rather speak of the "right" of God? We intend to ask the question in theological language and, in so doing, not to deny human rights (in the plural) from the political point of view in the broad sense of the term. We can perhaps ask the question in a different way. When the church, when Christians intend to render glory to God, to praise the Lord, indeed, to pray; when the church preaches the gospel and turns toward biblical witness, is that not to recognize the right of God as expressed in the *soli Deo gloria?* Now, right of God implies non-right of non-God, whether this be nature or man, even if the latter thinks he is subject of rights. If that is really so, if biblical witness and the preaching of the church proclaim the absolute right of God, every "human rights" approach has a first and unique basis in reference to absolute right, a reference to God—the God who reveals himself as subject of right.

Human rights appear as relative to the absolute right of God. They appear in the plural and are qualified. They are always something received or given and they are not at all natural. They are not glory but announce Glory. They are fruits of grace and witness to grace. Needless to say, that in no way lessens their importance; quite to the contrary, they are all the more important to the extent that the suppression of rights confronts us not only as an attack on the humanity of man, but rather—and especially—as a refusal of grace. One could not conceive of a church which would proclaim the grace of God in Jesus Christ and not at the same time strive to enlarge the realm of human rights, a necessary consequence of such grace. A purely theological question stems from this first assertion. The Christian approach to human rights can only build on the proper foundation, the order of redemption. That of course does not exclude reference to the order of creation, but it does prohibit becoming engaged in a search for the basis of human rights in the natural order, for the natural order is not at all the order of creation, but is rather what is called in Christian language sin. Historically, the natural order is always, or almost always, self-justifying, basing itself on situations of inequality, and therefore of injustice. It is not difficult to discern at the very foundation of naturalism a pattern of rich-poor, powerful-weak, even indeed, oppressor-oppressed. But the existence of this pattern serves precisely to prove that what is "natural" for the one who is rich and powerful is not at all natural for the one who is poor and weak, although the latter does not and cannot act except in the hope of reversing the situation—the hope of an opposite inequality. It is precisely that which renders problematical the universality of the "Universal" Declaration of Human Rights—besides, of course, its Western nature. Article 4 is "naturally" read very differently depending on which side of the rich-poor dichotomy one is on; and we can say the same about Article 17.

The search for the theological basis of human rights in the order of redemption takes history and present historical reality into account, but precisely because of that fact, it requires the action of liberation which expresses itself in rights. In large areas of today's world, it is quite simply tragic to say that all men are born free and with the same dignity and the same rights. The order of redemption requires us to say that all of us are called to be free in Jesus Christ, which is tantamount to saying that liberation is a requirement of the gospel. That is why the thoughts which follow are above all a Christological approach.

II. A Christological Approach

A. *Jesus Christ is the revelation of the right of God.*

> Thesis: God in Jesus Christ reveals himself as the objective reality of the freedom of the new man and as a result establishes human rights as a relational expression of human liberation.

1. By a decision of the absolute freedom of God (Gal. 4:4) is produced in the history of the world the event the gospel describes as Emmanuel (Matt. 1:23). It is not a matter, therefore, of *a* divine revelation, but of *the* revelation of God in the non-divine-in-itself, which is by that very fact transcended. The freedom of God is manifested in transcendence, not as a religious or theological category, but in an event which can be called transcendent because it transcended with its divinity the non-divine realm. Freedom is not therefore an ideal transcendent category, but the transcendent event which transcends the non-free milieu by freeing it for freedom. Emmanuel, God with us, is an impossibility, and therefore without recognition, an impossibility made possible by the freedom of God who thereby manifests his right. God is not God because he is Emmanuel; but, because he is Emmanuel (offense, stumbling block; 1 Pet. 2:6-8), he reveals himself as God in freedom and subject of right. God cannot be God with us, but in so being, he shows himself to be God—the free God who shows his right.

2. Jesus Christ is God in his freedom for himself and for us. Precisely because he is Emmanuel, subject of right, who transcends the non-divine milieu of the non-right, he establishes rights at the very center of non-right. In biblical language that is called "covenant." In this sense covenant is the liberating event by which non-right becomes subject of right. This covenant is "in my blood" (1 Cor. 11:25), that is, human rights are a reality by the fact that every human being— every creature—is placed before and in the liberating event of Jesus Christ, Emmanuel. By the covenant of liberation, man is man in God, subject of right, and in that way becomes one who has rights in the freedom of children of God.

3. The covenant of liberation is the event which liberates and reconciles (2 Cor. 5:19ff.) in four aspects of reconciliation: man with man, man with himself, man with nature, and man with God. Precisely because human rights are not a matter of something which refers to any simple aspect of being human—whether social, religious, or any other—but rather to the totality of being human, they have a range in Jesus Christ in the political realm (reconciliation of man with man), the psychological realm (man with himself), in men's relation with his environment (man with nature), and finally in the whole realm of life experience: faith (man with God). Although that idea needs more development, it must be emphasized here that one can find no other foundation than that which has been laid, Jesus Christ (1 Cor. 3:11).

4. The reconciling event of Emmanuel is in itself what the Christian faith designates as salvation. Salvation is therefore a liberating event situated in history, history transcended by God in his freedom. To be saved is to enter into a relationship of such a kind that the "I" (object) which has been saved is a subject "I" acting in freedom, which has been received and with rights which have themselves been received. Through these rights which he has received, the relational expression of human liberation, man is not object but subject of history. That is his liberty and that is his right, since he has been the object of the liberating event—Emmanuel—of the grace of the free God.

B. *Jesus Christ is the revelation of human rights.*

Thesis: Jesus of Nazareth, the Son of God, is the free man in communion with the Father; communion which he reveals in obedience even unto death and resurrection. As a result, each man and woman is called to freedom in communion with the Father and with other men and women in the covenant of Jesus Christ, who died and was resurrected.

1. In the Christian meaning of the term, human rights do not stem from the fact that man is man, but that man is in the communion of the Father and with other persons in Jesus Christ. If it is true (as we suggested above) that rights have reality only in freedom, we must place ourselves in relation to the liberating event of Jesus Christ in order to find the source of rights which are the result of it. For the revelation of freedom in Jesus Christ is experiencing communion with the Father and with his people—from which one can in no way exclude even those who condemned him. Precisely because the communion of life with the Father is contradicted by the negative communion of those who are opposed to Jesus Christ, the new man reveals his freedom in obedience for the salvation of others.

2. The availability of Jesus Christ for the other person makes of that other person one who receives the right to be in relationship with Jesus. In other words, the availability of Jesus humanizes man according to the new creation. That other person for whom Jesus makes himself available has not received "natural rights" which would make one subject of rights which no one but Jesus could recognize; rather, in encounter with Jesus, as object of the right of Jesus, humanity (in indignity) is invested with a dignity which makes a human being a relational subject of right.

44

3. Jesus, subject to the right of God, reveals in his encounter with human beings (individually and collectively) that human rights—in the usual sense of the term, as, for example, in the UN Declaration—are a cultural approach, not a "natural right." That is the case because only a cultural approach can define natural as natural, but above all because the dignity-investing encounter with Jesus Christ makes natural and cultural relative and, as it were, obliterates them.

4. Dignity received in indignity is the basis of freedom and therefore also of human rights which in the Christian faith ought not to be understood as "right of," but much more profoundly as "right for." In other words, freedom and the rights which are its consequence do not appear as categorical attributes of the mammal man, but rather in the acts of liberation which make of the mammal man, man in the image of the new man, Jesus Christ. Freedom—and therefore rights—are achieved in obedience.

C. *Man has received rights in Jesus Christ, the new Man.*

Thesis: Through the covenant of reconciliation in Jesus Christ, a person receives the dignity of being child of the God who frees him or her, and therefore the right of service for the liberation of every creature in the communion of God the Creator, Redeemer, and Savior.

1. The refusal of the service which liberates (and one must admit the possibility of error in understanding "liberation," a possibility that in no way justifies inhibition which would be, properly speaking, sin), in whatever realm of individual and social life, is a refusal of the freedom which has been received. The "yoke of bondage" (Gal. 5:1), which can be hidden under the most diverse cultural forces, from "religion" to "fine arts," from "politics" to "economics," is an idolatrous refusal of Jesus Christ, in which men and women face the world which surrounds them and face themselves as subjects of right. In this sense, every tyranny (yoke of bondage)—religious, political, of whatever sort—is idolatrous and presents "another gospel."

2. The right to service for the liberation of every creature in the reconciliation of Jesus Christ appears in various forms, with the emphasis placed on the individual servant. All are based primarily on the social concept of people. But the essential element of all is their final and principal reference to creatures of God who are called to freedom and await the manifestation of children of God (Rom. 8:19ff.).

3. Rights which have been received in Jesus Christ are an active

event *in* history and in no way an historical fact which is acquired in a cultural tradition. In other words, rights, whatever they are, are an act of liberation and not a fundamental property of the individual.

4. As a result, the individual as well as the human community (people) must be freed, that is, reconciled with self in the communion of Jesus Christ. We are concerned here not only with the "religious" dimension, which would place that liberation in "trans-history," but with the present reality of historical man in the double character of man and of woman (*sexus-sectus!*) in dialogue with the environment which makes them into an "I."

5. The reference to the environment not only as "place" but also as part of the "I" prevents all idealization of rights in the sense of the liberal tradition, for that environment is not Paradise. At the same time, the reference to the environment points out the principal difference between humanist idealism and what Christians understand by the dignity of the children of God,[1] even if in other respects the language used by humanist idealism and the community of the faith is similar.

III. Some Concluding Remarks

I have intentionally tried to mention specific "rights" for it seems to me that what we ought to consider is theological criticism of the Western tradition. The right of expression and of assembly are, in our tradition, *defensive historical rights.* That does not mean that we should give them up: quite otherwise. But we must remember that their active reality is always limited by political powers in the broad sense of the term. They could be truly realized only in utopia, and since experience proves that we are not there, they become the property of those who have the means to exercise them. That constitutes privilege for those who are privileged and not service for the liberation of the underprivileged.

The right to private property, dear as it may be to Western tradition, is even more clearly defensive. It is very closely related to the principle of the legitimacy of self-defense, which seems to be beyond all question in Western culture and perhaps in all cultures, but which in my opinion has no theological justification. Without entering now into the discussion of that question, which would lead us too far afield, we can take as a working hypothesis the biblical tenet of the

[1] Cf. Rubem Alves, *¿ Religión, opio o instrumento de liberación?*, p. 133.

46

salvation of the other person rather than self-defense—the safeguarding of my life as a primary and indisputable value. Even if we accept that only as a provisional hypothesis, it follows that the right to private property is at least disputable for theological reasons as well as for reasons of a materialistic dialectic of history.

There are, however, some practical questions which must be considered in a theological analysis of human rights. We shall point out three:

A. *The question of human rights is an open one, and it must remain open.*

The first part of this statement is self-evident, and it would seem unnecessary to comment on it. It is clear that human rights, even in the sense of the philosophy of the UN Declaration, have only been declared, not experienced, in the greater part of the world. But what one must always bear in mind is that human rights can only be theoretical because they are established on the basis of a non-historical philosophy. They do not take reality into account; rather, they imagine it ideally. But if we wish to remain within reality we cannot forget either the programmatic dimension of the ministry of reconciliation or its historical dimension. To neglect the former would be to fall into an historical determinism that even primitive Marxist dialectic cannot escape (in spite of the efforts of Engels!); to neglect the second would mean entering into a type of idealistic Manicheism—as often happens in Christianity.

The real question seems to be the search for criteria for human rights. And these criteria can only be found in changing historical reality, even if they do not belong to history but to the event which transcended history. Possibly one will sometimes find oneself repeating certain expressions recognizable as liberal humanism, but the meaning of these will be quite different. These criteria are theologically based on "freedom for" and not on "freedom from." They cannot be defensive or they can be defensive only, but they must permit the humanization of men and women in the sense of the new creation in Jesus Christ.

B. *Theologically, rights are a function of liberation.*

There is nothing more foreign to the event of Jesus Christ than the maintenance of the status quo. If Jesus Christ is truly the revelation of the right of God, no status quo can be maintained in the experience of the event of the right of God. The maintenance of the status quo—the rich-poor, powerful-weak pattern—seems, however, to be the result, if not the goal, of so-called human rights in the naturalist and rationalist perspective characteristic of usual declarations, particularly the UN Declaration. Theologically, that implies the negation of *solus Christus* to the advantage of a certain person who can exercise his or her right and to the disadvantage of another person who cannot exercise it. The first is lord and the second is serf, a structure which is institutionalized and which developed in such a way that the rich individual or nation become richer by the day and the gap between rich and poor grows daily wider. Indirectly, that shows that the claim to the maintenance of the status quo always fails in history in one sense or another and that "human rights," which are always declared by the powerful side of the rich-poor pattern, are an *a posteriori* justification of the historical evolution of established structures. If rights are truly the relational manifestations of freedom, it is only in the process of liberation and in terms of it that rights have a real existence. Once again, it seems that the core is the alternative "freedom from" or "freedom for."

C. Right and violence

A third question appears immediately: that of violence. At first glance, right and violence seem to be opposed to each other, but that is only a superficial approach characteristic of the rationalist idealism of human rights declarations. Theologically, one must ask oneself what the violence of Jesus Christ is; and we shall soon see that the incarnation is the violent expression par excellence of the affirmation of the right of God. Such expressions as "eternity is in time," "the holy God dwells among the unholy," "the light shines in the darkness," "the kingdom is among us," are theological and biblical expressions of the violence of God manifesting his right. Evangelically, that violence is more than salutary; it is salvation itself—salvation which frees man and the entire creation in the new man, the firstborn of the new creation.

It is difficult to think of liberation without violence. The question is: which violence? This concerns more than a verbal choice; it concerns a choice that is lived, an inescapable choice of faith. Order, for example, is a type of violence; disorder another. The right to service for the liberation of the other person accepts the condition of violence in the faith of Jesus Christ and in the assurance of the faithful love of God, which also manifested itself violently in the incarnation, death, and resurrection of Jesus Christ for the salvation of others.

5. A North American Response

MARGRETHE B. J. BROWN and M. EUGENE OSTERHAVEN

Current thinking in the church about human rights has relatively recent origins. In essence "political theology" is as old as Augustine, and interest in liberation is as ancient as the biblical revelation. It was not until the Reformation of the sixteenth century that "the freedom of the Christian man"—afterwards in the Enlightenment "human rights"—became a household topic. Thrust aside because of the pressure of other, seemingly more urgent topics, these have again become serious concerns of the church. It has not been the older churches which have demonstrated their biblical relevance, however, but minority churches of the "Third World" for whose members they have assumed great importance. To them the whole church is indebted for calling attention to the many tendencies towards and forms of dehumanization under which children of God are forced to live. The cry for liberation and the accompanying demand for human rights voiced by these people serve other Christians as a gracious reminder of their own responsibility to institute and to engage in programs which are directed towards the achieving of those ends. Consideration of the theology of human rights and the theology of liberation is no optional matter for the people of God today, therefore, but a requirement laid before them by none other than the Lord of the church who, at the beginning of his ministry, announced that he had come "to preach good news to the poor . . . to proclaim release to the captives and recovering of sight to the blind, to set at liberty those who are oppressed, to proclaim the acceptable year of the Lord" (Luke 4:18f.).

Margrethe B. J. Brown is a lecturer in theology at the Lutheran Theological Seminary, Columbus, Ohio, and an ordained minister in the United Presbyterian Church. M. Eugene Osterhaven is professor of systematic theology, Western Theological Seminary, Holland, Michigan. The North American committee was chaired by the Editor of this volume.

I. The Basis of the Theology of Liberation and the Theology of Human Rights

A. The Theology of Liberation

1. The theology of liberation is the fruit of reflection on God's liberation of Israel from bondage in Egypt and of Christ's liberation of mankind from sin and its consequences through his life, death, and resurrection. Thus the event of liberation has preceded theory. God has saved and set his people free; afterwards they have reflected on the full meaning of their salvation.

2. The theology of liberation has arisen out of specific social, economic, and political conditions in which Christians who have come to know the freedom that is in Jesus Christ feel called to extend that freedom to the benefit of both the oppressed and oppressors.

3. The theology of liberation is a concrete response of Christians to the social and economic inequities which rob people of the possibility of developing those gifts which God has given them and subject them to other people in a condition of servitude. The theology of liberation is thus an attempt to understand God's salvation in Jesus Christ comprehensively so that it includes the whole life of men and women in society.

4. The church reformed according to the Word of God and ever aware of the need for renewal (*semper reformanda*) must be actively engaged in bringing the gospel of freedom in Jesus Christ to all people and in implementing that gospel of freedom in all of their social, economic, and political relationships.

B. The Theology of Human Rights

1. Scripture witnesses to the rights of God and of Jesus Christ who "bears the very stamp of his nature" (Heb. 1:3). Respect is due to human beings because Christ, in his incarnation, has identified himself with the human condition.

2. The concept of human rights arose in the Christianization of societies and states as the dignity of the human person came to be realized in politics and in law. This concept was endorsed by the United Nations in its Universal Declaration of Human Rights (1948), which has been recognized as an internationally binding statement.

3. Human rights are the tarnished reflection seen by secular man of the *imago dei*. They are what the world sees of the image of God

and that to which both Christians and non-Christians appeal in the struggle for liberation.

4. Human rights are those entitlements which God bestows upon those made in his image whereby they both treat other people and expect to be treated like children of God whose persons are loved and whose goods and reputations are honored and respected for the sake of Jesus Christ in whom all rights inhere.

5. Declarations of human rights are effective only insofar as there are men and women who are determined to take upon themselves the rights and duties of mankind and, for the sake of humanity, stand up for the oppressed. Freedom is real and effective only insofar as free persons intercede for the liberation of enslaved persons and both see themselves as children of God.

6. When in a time of conflict national security takes precedence over human rights so that these are violated, that fact should be acknowledged and those rights should be restored as soon as possible.

7. Inasmuch as a person is free only as he or she is bound to God, the source of all blessing, those persons and societies that neglect or reject him lose their freedom and may lose the privilege of exercising their rights.

8. The concept of human rights, once articulated, acquires new appreciation and requires fresh treatment in periods of oppression.

II. The Context of the Present Discussion of the Theology of Human Rights and the Theology of Liberation.

A. The good news as a liberating force in human lives and communities is being proclaimed where persons are suffering injustice at the hands of dominating forces. With faith and hope in Christ these oppressed people have received strength to reject the shackles of human bondage and to live as free children of God.

B. The theology of liberation as response to the proclamation of the good news of freedom in Jesus Christ is a legitimate and necessary articulation of the full meaning of the gospel. It should be accepted as such by the whole church as the latter seeks to obey God's will that every person be made complete in Jesus Christ (Col. 1:28).

C. The theology of liberation arises from the cry of ethnic and cultural minorities: as, for example, in North America, of black

Americans who by faith are discovering their identity as full citizens of the kingdom of God; of Chicanos and Latin Americans; of North American Indians, Eskimos, French Canadians, Asian Americans, and others who by grace are finding strength within their respective heritages, in spite of the dominant culture, to live as free men and women before God.

D. The theology of liberation arises from the cry of Third World peoples who, after centuries of exploitation and injustice, are demanding acceptance by the whole church as brothers and sisters in Jesus Christ. Made free by him, they claim for themselves and their fellows full citizenship in this world and in the world to come.

E. The theology of liberation is a response to other oppression: to that of women who after centuries of subjugation now claim their full role as participants in all of human society; to that of the handicapped, the old, and the young whom our social, economic, political, and judicial systems have marginalized and abused.

F. The call for liberation also comes from the midst of the dominating group where persons in faith perceive their own enslavement by the oppressive system of which they are a part; persons who yearn in Christ to identify with those who suffer oppression, knowing not only the victory of the resurrection but also the death of the cross and its inevitable pain.

III. The Meaning of Liberation

A. Liberation is freedom given by the Lord Jesus Christ from servitude to sin and its personal and social consequences, and the ability, through the power of his Holy Spirit, to live a life of obedience, gratitude, and joy for God and one's fellow men and women.

B. Liberation thus includes release from any social situation which prevents the emergence and growth of love among people; from the dominance of one person over another, of one group over another, of a group over an individual, or an individual over a group.

C. Liberation frees human life from isolation and alienation, from pride and prejudice, from hatred and fear, and from all forms of debilitating sin.

D. Liberation frees human beings from the powers and principalities that distort the relationships within communities and history, and from the corporations and systems which negate human development and personality.

E. Liberation frees human beings from the false and selfish desires for the survival of one's self and one's kind at the expense of others, thereby distorting the promise of human life in the fullness of the image of God.

F. Liberation frees human beings from the false dependence upon material goods that robs them of their true nature as children of God who are dependent upon one another.

G. A person is free when one believes that one's personal worth and destiny are secured by the grace of God.

H. The personal liberation which is the fullest fruit of sanctification is the perfection of love which triumphs even when violated.

I. Liberation is the knowledge that we are not locked into a situation in which there is no capacity for change, but that by a divine, radical surgery we and our fellow human beings may alter conditions, grow in the knowledge and grace of God, and help secure those rights to which every person is entitled.

IV. The Call of the Christian
to Share in the Struggle for Liberation

A. Since Christians are members of one another and of the same body of Christ (1 Cor. 12:12–27), they share each other's joys and sorrows. When one member suffers, all members suffer together (vs. 26). Hence, no Christian may remain indifferent when other Christians (or, because of our common human dignity, when non-Christians) are denied their God-given human rights and are oppressed.

B. As all Christian believers are called to share in the struggle of the oppressed of the earth for liberation, so also Christian theology, in the face of admitted difficulty in speaking for others, must articulate the yearnings and the cries of "the wretched of the earth" so that others may hear and understand.

C. Inasmuch as all men and women share in the quest for liberation even while some do not recognize the source of this blessing, Christians are with them as fellow-pilgrims and participants in the common struggle. In grateful appreciation of their efforts and humble recognition of their own failures, Christians strive with them in every legitimate undertaking to improve our common life, hopeful that they too will come to know the Lord who alone can set them free.

D. "All that we call political theologies, or theologies of hope, of revolution, of liberation, are not worth one single true gesture of solidarity with the exploited social classes. They are not worth one single act of faith, love, and hope, committed and actively engaged to liberate man from everything that dehumanizes him or which prevents him from living according to the will of the Father."[1]

V. The Sustaining Hope

A. The theology of liberation is the theology of the future, for the kingdom of God and of his Son is the future of the true humanity of men and women.

B. The theology of liberation is the explication of the emergence of the new person in Christ and of his true church on earth. It is the eschatological hope of the kingdom.

C. The theology of liberation and the theology of human rights provide dignity for those who suffer and enable them to speak in courage and in truth even while they reject the cause of unjust suffering in the present inasmuch as they know that the future victory is the Lord's, both now and then.

D. The theology of liberation and the theology of human rights proclaim the possibility of the courage to face any future regardless of the oppressions of the past; thus people may assume responsibility for their own histories and social interrelationships.

E. The theology of liberation and the theology of human rights presuppose the freedom to enter into dialogue with other individuals and groups of people, trusting those of different cultures and expressions of life-style who are also in search of mutual respect and a future of human relationships free of suspicion, distrust, hatred, and war.

F. The Christian faith therefore is essentially a firm confidence in the eventual completion of the saving work of the God who is active in history. All human effort that serves the cause of liberation and of human rights takes place in the context of the coming kingdom of God and receives from it its meaning and reward.

[1] Gustavo Gutierrez, *A Theology of Liberation*, p. 308.

6. Pressing the Claims, Interpreting the Cries

HUGH A. KOOPS

"We are constantly talking about rights. The only right we have is to be damned. We have no rights before God." "The Bible does not speak about rights and liberties, which are due to mankind by nature, but of a justice and a liberation, which are given to man by God." Such observations, adequate though they be within their context, invite and require an apology for a discussion on the theological basis for human rights. They constitute my apology for beginning with an apology.

The first of the difficulties in dealing with the theological basis of human rights concerns the nature of theology; subsequent problems are internal to the theological enterprise.

To seek a theological basis for human rights, this criticism runs, is already to disclose the poverty of theology. If human rights indeed have a theological base, it should not be necessary to look for it. But the Bible does not speak of human rights. Those statements which most clearly specify human rights, the Declaration of Independence, the French National Assembly's Declaration of Rights of Man and of Citizens, and the Universal Declaration of Human Rights, are political rather than confessional statements. They have their origins in the rationalistic and democratic tradition rather than in the Christian faith. To seek a theological basis for human rights is to christen the illegitimate child rather hurriedly after it is learned that he will not be an embarrassment.

If the test of a hypothesis is its predictability, if the proof of an ideology is preparation for the future, then it may be admitted that theology does not fare well by human rights. Theology has a long history; "the concept of human rights is relatively young in the

Hugh A. Koops is professor of church and community, New Brunswick Theological Seminary, New Brunswick, New Jersey. The author commends the reader to the article, "A Theological Approach to Moral Rights," by Joseph L. Allen, pp. 119–141, in The Journal of Religious Ethics, Vol. II (Spring 1974).

world's history, and its implementation in human social and political life is even more recent." There is a paucity of literature on theology and human rights.

Should theology be seen as an ideology, as a system of thought, this criticism is cogent. There are, however, responses. Theologies, as systems of thought, may have utilized symbols and categories other than "human rights" or concerned themselves with other, possibly more important, issues. The leisure required to produce theologies may have precluded class participation in the struggle for the definition of human rights. Other excuses can also be invented.

However, should theology be seen as a way of thinking, this criticism loses some of its cogency. The pretensions of theology may be embarrassed by the absence of a consideration of human rights, but the process of theology cannot be judged irrelevant. The inquiry into the theological basis stands; the term *basis* uncovers the confession of faith that theology is basic. The quest for the basis is not the attempt to get in on a good thing, but to search for the fundamental relationships between human rights and the manner in which Christians perceive them, participate in them, and respond to them. Theology, as a way of thinking, can confess that "the practice of liberation has preceded the writing of theory. Yahweh's liberation of Israel and Christ's liberation of men preceded confession." Theologians, not theology, must bear the brunt of this complaint.

Within theology itself, however, there seem to be some reasons for avoiding the discussion of human rights. These reasons must also, though briefly, be addressed.

Can the *creature* have rights? Because God is creator, ruler, and redeemer, should we not say that no one has rights but God alone? To predicate rights of man is to threaten the freedom of God. Persons do not have rights; they have only privileges. The creature can never press his rights against God. The clay cannot make demands of the potter. Humanity exists by the creative decision of God. Man is no more entitled to three score years and ten than he is to one. People are the most privileged of creatures, but they are no more than privileged.

But what is the relevance of rights in the context of creation? To say that God alone has rights says little. Against whom must God press his claim to his rights? We say nothing when we say that God alone has rights.

And if God is creator, and the creative decision rests with him, he can grant rights as well as existence. Such rights, to be sure, cannot be seen as absolute rights. They exist only by the graciousness of God.

But such existence is all that can be claimed of the existence of man himself. With creation God has "covenanted" with man, has promised man his steadfast love. Not everything that man might want is promised by God, but man has the right to God's steadfast love. Moreover, the concrete display of God's love in the provision of space, of work, of companionship, of self-identity, and of worship begins the specification of steadfast love within the conditions of human existence.

Only within the transaction of creation, the interchange of promises, can we speak of God's right to man's adoration and obedience. Only within this implicit covenant can we speak of man's right to God's steadfast love. And this human right need never be pressed. To press this right would be the very indication of unbelief.

The existence of this possibility raises the second objection. Can the *sinner* have rights? Granted the right of God to man's obedience and the right of man to God's steadfast love, were those rights not forfeited when that love was challenged by unbelief, disobedience, and pride? It is well and good to say that human rights participate in the gracious bestowal of God to display his concern for man. But man's claim on God has been forfeited. This right to his love has been lost in the disruption and distortion of sin. He is barred from the garden, his work becomes laborious, his identity masked by defensiveness, and his relationship with kin and God broken by blame.

Nonetheless, he continues to exist as man. The garden is guarded by cherubim, thorns and thistles bring sweat to his brow, hatred and death penetrate his family, but God does not abandon him. God's promise of steadfast love continues; without its continuation man could not survive, but with its continuation man retains his right to God's love.

Moreover, within the conditions of sinful existence, human rights become necessary. Only within sinful existence can their claims be pressed. Only in a fallen world need they be exercised. Where human rights are not violated, they are not evident. Just as man need not express his right to God's love unless he distrusts the love he receives, so man need not express his rights (finite though they be) until their exercise is challenged by others.

Man's vision of innocence, thus, is precisely disclosed when his legitimate rights are defended. Here he illustrates his ambiguity, his habitation between essence and existence.

To speak of human rights, therefore, is neither to compromise God's freedom in creation nor his judgment in condemnation. To speak of human rights is to express his freedom and his judgment. Human rights reflect what it is to love with a love which is not steadfast but knows a steadfast love. Human rights express the commitment of God in love toward his creatures.

There is another objection, internal to theology, to human rights: Are human rights *natural?* To assert the existence of natural human rights, or just plain natural rights, seems to say that these rights are absolute. They are rooted in nature. As natural, they cannot be gainsaid. Natural rights are absolute rights. But since human rights are not absolute, human rights are not natural. Rather, they are supernatural, the gift of grace.

However, before we purchase this rejection of natural rights, we might examine why the assertion is made. There may be no Catholic bugaboo hiding behind the "natural." Actually, the preservation of the term preserves but two elements: (1) human rights belong to all who are by nature human; and (2) human rights are not simply created or conferred by individual or by social decision.

In this context natural has nothing to do with the "natural" as over against the "supernatural." It is simply a descriptive device which attributes such rights to all men quite independent of their knowledge or their choice. We need not object, as long as we remember that our nature is to exist wholly by the grace of God, and we are to be obligated to God in all we have and are, our natural rights included. Natural rights originate in God, they extend to all men, and they are not portable by human fiat. Such rights belong to all persons. Even where misused, as in foolish speaking or in false worship, they are not to be constrained by others. To make them subject to human decision would be to violate the freedom of another, to treat the other as less than human by nature. Or to subject others to human decision would be to treat the other as if one were "more" than human, "to be as God."

One last, apologetic, section remains. Since the Christian ethic is obviously an ethic of obligation or *duty,* how can human *rights* play any role of significance? The Christian life finds its paradigm in the sacrificial love of Christ. Can there be any room for agapic love where rights prevail?

Here, again, the problem is illusory. Our most fundamental duties arise because of the rights of others. Only when we respond to their rights are we responsive to our duties. Agapic love never denies, but persistently transforms, human rights.

A series of possible situations can demonstrate this apology. When

58

we are faced with the competing claims between two or more parties, we cannot ignore their rights. Along with an analysis of the facts comes a determination of their respective rights. The loving thing to do may well be more than the determination of the right thing to do. It will never be less. Love's concerns are not attained apart from the concerns of justice.

The situation becomes more difficult, however, when the competing claims emerge between oneself and others. Is it not, in this situation, more loving to abandon one's own rights, as well as one's own interests, to serve the claims of the other? Before the hasty response, note first that the rights one claims may well be representative of the rights of others. To give up one's own rights may thus be doing an injustice to the others one represents as well.

Proceeding to more difficult ground, the situation may involve competing claims between oneself and the other, with no additional involvements. By eliminating the representation of others, we are clearly in a different situation. Here, too, the abandonment of rights may include the abandonment of duty. The maintenance of one's rights may be the necessary means of serving the other (for example, by instructing him in his duties as well as his rights), of presenting the realities of human existence to the other.

One additional qualification must still be considered. Should there be no others involved, and no useful consequences in maintaining one's rights for the sake of the complainant, one must still see himself as he is. The self should be known to self as a creature of God, good, of worth in his own sight, and never merely a means for others. To accept creation, which demands including others, also includes the acceptance of oneself. The decision, which can indeed be justified, to be for the other a means rather than an end must not entail the denial of self along with the abandonment of rights. To go a step further, if there are no defenders of human rights, Christians may find their most difficult duty to be the protection and defense of their most disinterested right.

The possession of a right and the exercise of the right must be distinguished. Not all rights need always be exercised in order to be maintained. But human rights, even one's own rights, have an intimate connection with sacrificial love which self-sacrifice does not always accommodate. If rights are to be seen as gifts from God, and if duties are to be seen as commands from God, we cannot forget the precedence of the gift over the command.

Our journey toward "the theological basis of human rights" has thus far found us moving slowly forward while looking backward, apologetically. We haven't gone as far as we might have wished had we set out more directly. But now, knowing where we have been, we have nonetheless travelled considerably. The journey ahead is not as long as if we were to start all over from the beginning.

First of all, the creation of man has established man as a *bearer of rights*. To be created man, in the image of God, is to bear human rights. That right which man possesses in relation to the God who made him is the right to his steadfast love. The exercise of love's reciprocity, expressed in man's reflection of God's image, is impressed upon creation in the duality of sexual interdependence for human destiny. Each, in love, is subject to the other. The divine creative love is imaged in the human recreative love which embodies all persons as persons. To be human is to love and to be loved in turn. To love is to know oneself loved by God. To be loved by God is to know oneself never to be abandoned by God, and always to be in the possession of the right to be loved.

The fall, resulting from man's inability to cope with his finitude, curtails the boundaries of human existence and blurs man's vision. Man's world shrinks, his life becomes burdensome. The reciprocity of love is constrained; even the family is more than love can unite. But the right to be loved, if not the capacity to love, abides. It is rooted in the steadfast love of God.

The limits of love's capacity demand the control of hate's destruction. Hate is barred from eternal life; it will never approach love's ultimacy. The reciprocity of love is diluted, and man's right to be free in his loving is reduced to man's right to be free. Even this freedom, like man's love, is constrained by finitude. Finite man's freedom can be maximized only in the equal right of all men to be free for love, the equal duty of all men to be bound to serve. When rights and duties immobilize man, the criterion of mutual love becomes equality.

The human right can thus be described as "the equal right of all men to be free." To be denied this right is to be deemed as one who does not count as others count. Humanity's rights are denied when anyone is treated as a means to the end of another. No one may have less than an equal right to freedom. This is why slavery is wrong, why coerced segregation is wrong, why discrimination is wrong. Allowing the exceptions of sinking lifeboats and burning theatres, the human rights of free speech and free worship, the pursuit of happiness and the resistance to oppression, the search for love and the results of work witness to what it means to be human in normal circumstances.

The biblical witness gives testimony to "the right of all to be equally free." It is most dramatic where the right is not only pronounced, but particularly effected for those whose rights have been deprived. From years of slavery in Egypt, a people who were no people became a people by the Lord's almighty hand. In his deliverance from bondage he gave the law with its provisions against murder, adultery, stealing, false witness, and coveting, all implying respect for and nurturance of human life. Nathan rebuked the king David with an appeal to pity for the helpless. Amos berated Israel for neglecting the widows and the orphans. The priority of persons over requirements is most explicit in the gospels. "The Sabbath was made for man, and not man for the Sabbath." The full identification of God's intention within human experience is found in the incarnation. God himself joined the oppressed, moving from crowded inns in ancestral communities where taxes need be paid to a crucifixion outside the city as a common criminal. And witness the ultimate acclamation of man's "equal rights with all to be free" in the clear identification by the apostles of those who had crucified Jesus, thus forfeiting their rights to be free, but the removal of the legal demands against them by the raising of the victim from the grave!

It is obvious that human rights are never born in solitude. Their existence and their exercise assumes community. All too often these rights were exercised in the smallest of communities: our family, our friends, our neighborhood, our people, our nation. Christian tradition, clearly building on the Hebraic experience, came to see with the eighth-century prophets that God is the creator of the universe. Rights certainly were to extend, as love was to extend, both to the neighbor and the enemy. The alien stranger occupies middle ground, as foreign as the enemy yet as near as the neighbor. And Israel was regularly given two reasons for recognizing the rights of the stranger: (1) Israel had herself been a stranger and a sojourner in the land of Egypt, and (2) the Lord himself always loved strangers and sojourners. Paul taught Christians to confess the Christ as Lord of all. All are one in Christ Jesus.

Moreover, human rights have a history. They do not exist independent of a past or a future. They express what it means to be human in specific social and historical relationships. Consider a variety of rights illustrated over the range of biblical history: the right of the slave to be freed after six years, the right of the first-born to the inheritance, the right to protection from vengeance within the cities of refuge, the right to a wife after seven years of labor, the right to have a debt repaid, the right to a fair trial by the honored judges at the city gate, the right of Paul to receive support from the churches for his work.

Few would insist that these rights should be preserved today. Some of these rights are peculiar rights, established through the special terms of certain personal covenants. Others are general rights. The general rights were also seen as the products of covenant. Historically, these general rights were like special rights in their origin within a covenant made by God with his people. Functionally, they served as general rights, holding all to their obligations.

These rights reflect a moral fabric, a social ethos. This is not to conclude that human rights are simply conventional, that any society could choose to reject these conventions and consequently exist apart from the acknowledgment of basic human rights. Rather, the ethos will determine what is to be shared equally among all. But the inalienable right is that each possesses "the equal right of all to be free."

To illustrate: the right to work was a right seldom required in a pre-industrial society where the tools for labor were simply and easily made and readily available. The right to work became crucial only when the means of production were no longer available to workers and access to work was necessary for human survival. The particular form of a human right will vary widely from ethos to ethos. The "equal right of all to be free" should be maintained in all.

One observation concludes our treatment of the relationship of human rights to community and history. Because the particular form of human rights is so tightly interwoven with the ethos of a society, human rights cannot be left to personal impulses. Human rights are the concern of institutional policy as well as personal relations. Jesus began his ministry in Nazareth with his commentary on Isaiah:

> The spirit of the Lord is upon me because he has anointed me;
> he has sent me to announce good news to the poor,
> to proclaim release for prisoners and recovery of sight for the blind;
> to let the broken victims go free,
> to proclaim the year of the Lord's favor (Luke 4:18f.).

His former acquaintances heard him gladly, as would the multitude later. Even when he continued, "Today in your very hearing this text has come true," they admired him. But they became infuriated with him when he reminded them of God's inclusion of a widow in Sarepta and a general from Syria within his grace. This broad extension of human rights they could not tolerate, particularly because they knew he wasn't asking them simply to care for a widow for a day, or wave a friendly greeting to a visiting Syrian. They knew he announced the revival of the honored institution of the jubilee. And that could mean, if Sidonians and Syrians are to be included, that the return of the land and the remission of debts could lead, not simply to the removal of the Roman occupation, but a social and political and economic reconstruction of society which excluded no one. Human rights, to include the poor, the prisoners, the blind, and the victims, especially if foreigners are included, are expensive.

There is a straight line from Nazareth to North America.

As for the citizens of Nazareth, so there is for us little likelihood of participation in the ongoing definition of human rights for the forthcoming future (my phrase for the time between the present and the establishment of the post-industrial, non-expansionist economy which is to come). The motivation for the redefinition of particular human rights comes from the oppressed who are in covenant with the liberating Lord of history.

We have another, and more difficult, task. We are not in Egypt, not in the Upper Room. We are either in the wilderness, complaining about the absence of the condiments of the connoisseur (the leeks, the onions, the melons, the cucumbers, and the garlic, not to overlook all the free fish) or we are shouting "Hosanna" to some civic religion hero. We are abusing privilege, and prostituting human rights.

Our task has two dimensions. The first is to press the claims of equality on personal practice and social policy. The second is to interpret the cries of oppressed people as the Word of God in our time. In the process we must learn what few have accomplished. We must learn how, in the defense of human rights, to surrender privilege. We must look for the kingdom in the cross of Christ. And without God's help, we will never get the camel through the needle's eye.

7. Black Theology on Revolution, Violence, and Reconciliation

JAMES H. CONE

How is Christianity related to the black revolution in America? The answer to this question is not easy since we live in a white society that emphasizes the seeming discontinuity between "blackness-revolution" and the gospel of Jesus. Black consciousness as expressed in black power is by definition revolutionary in white America, if by revolution we mean a sudden, radical, and complete change; or as Jürgen Moltmann puts it: "a transformation in the foundations of a system— whether of economics, of politics, or morality, or of religion."[1] In America "law and order" means obedience to the law of white people, and "stability" means the continuation of the present in the light of the past—defined and limited by George Washington, Abraham Lincoln, and Richard Nixon. Revolution then means anything that challenges the "sacredness" of the past which is tantamount to usurping the rule of white oppressors. That is why J. Edgar Hoover described the Black Panthers as the most serious internal threat to the American way of life.

But for black people, revolution means that blacks no longer accept the history of white people as the key to their existence in the future. It also means they are prepared to do what is necessary in order to assure that their present and future existence will be defined by black visions of reality. We believe, as Ernst Bloch puts it: "Things can be otherwise. That means: things can also *become* otherwise: in the direction of evil, which must be avoided, or in the direction of good, which would have to be promoted."[2] The black revolution

---

[1] *Religion, Revolution and the Future*, tr. Douglas Meeks (New York: Scribners, 1969), p. 131.
[2] "Man as Possibility" in *Cross Currents*, XVIII, 3 (Summer 1968), 274.

James H. Cone is professor of theology at Union Theological Seminary, New York. This paper was originally published in the Union Seminary Quarterly Review, Vol. XXXI, No. 1, Fall 1975, pp. 5-14.

involves tension between the actual and the possible, the "white past" and the "black future," and the black community accepting the responsibility of defining the world according to its "open possibilities."

Moltmann is right: "Truth is revolutionary," that is, truth involves "discovering that the world can be changed and that nothing has to remain as it has been."[3] White oppressors cannot share in this future reality as defined by the black revolution. Indeed, we blacks assume that the white position of unauthorized power as expressed in the racist character of every American institution—churches and seminaries not excluded!—renders white oppressors incapable of understanding what black humanity is, and it is thus incumbent upon us as black people to become "revolutionaries for blackness," rebelling against all who enslave us. With Marcus Garvey, we say, "Any sane man, race or nation that desires freedom must first of all think in terms of blood."

In contrast to the revolutionary thrust of black power, Christianity usually is not thought of as being involved in radical change. It has been identified with the status quo, a condition that encourages oppression and not human liberation. Some black religionists, like Howard Thurman and Albert Cleage, say that the Apostle Paul must bear a heavy responsibility for the theological justification of human oppression. It was Paul who admonished slaves to be obedient to their masters; in Romans 13, he urged all men to be subject to the state. While it is possible to question the use of Paul in this context, especially in view of the radical eschatological vision of first-century Christians and the contrasting differences between the social and political situation of Paul's time and ours, we cannot deny that later theologies used Paul as a theological justification of economic and political oppression. Indeed, it can be said that when Constantine made Christianity the official religion of the Roman state (replacing the public state sacrifices), the gospel of Jesus became a religious justification of the interests of the state. Theologians began to equate the immoral with the unlawful and slavery with the sins of the slaves. As Augustine put it: Slavery was due to the sinfulness of the slaves. Therefore, like Paul, he admonished "slaves to be subject to their masters . . . ," serving them "with a good-heart and a good-will. . . ."[4]

During the Middle Ages, Thomas Aquinas took his cue from

[3] Moltmann, *op. cit.,* p. 132.
[4] *The City of God*, tr. Marcus Dods (New York: Modern Library, 1950), p. 694.

Augustine. "Slavery among men is natural," wrote Thomas. "The slave, in regard to his master, is an instrument. . . . Between a master and his slave there is a special right of domination."[5]

The idea that the slave should be obedient to his master and should not seek to change his civil status through revolutionary violence is found throughout the Christian tradition. In Protestant Christianity, this emphasis is found in Martin Luther and his definition of the state as the servant of God. That was why he condemned the Peasants' revolt, saying that "nothing can be more poisonous, hurtful, or devilish than a rebel." He equated killing a rebel peasant with the killing of a mad dog.[6]

It is unfortunate that Protestant Christianity did not offer a serious challenge to modern slavery in Europe and America. Calvinism seemed especially suited for America with its easy affinity for capitalism and slavery. While John Wesley, the founder of Methodism, did not endorse slavery, he appeared to be more concerned about a warm heart than an enslaved body. And his evangelist friend, George White-field, publicly defended the slave institution in Georgia. It is a sad fact that Protestants not only tolerated slavery but many actually encouraged it.

The same emphasis is found in modern Catholicism. It rarely defended the interests of the oppressed. In 1903 Pope Pius X clarified the Catholic position:

> Human society as established by God is made up of unequal elements . . . . Accordingly, it is in conformity with the order of human society as established by God that there be rulers and ruled, employers and employees, learned and ignorant, nobles and plebeians.[7]

In 1943, in a similar vein, Pope Pius XII advised the Italian workers that

> Salvation and justice are not to be found in revolution but in evolution through concord. Violence has always achieved only destruction, not construction; the kindling of passions, not their pacification; the accumulation of hate and ruin, not the reconciliation of the contending parties. And it has reduced men and parties to the difficult task of rebuilding, after sad experience, on the ruins of discord.[8]

---

[5] Cited in Roger Garaudy, *From Anathema to Dialogue* (New York: Vintage, 1968), p. 98.
[6] Cited in Roland Bainton, *Here I Stand* (Nashville: Abingdon, 1950), p. 280.
[7] Cited in Garaudy, *op. cit.*, p. 98.
[8] George Celestin, "A Christian Looks at Revolution" in Marty and Peerman (eds.), *New Theology No. 6* (New York: Macmillan, 1969), p. 69.

We may conclude then that the essential differences between Protestants and Catholics do not lie in their stand on revolution. Both agree that the state has divine sanction and thus violent revolution must be condemned. And if there are rare exceptions in which violence can be justified, these exceptions do not apply to black people and their liberation struggle in America. In regard to the black revolution, Protestants and Catholics alike stand solidly on their tradition. It seems that the most "radical" comment coming from the white churches is: "We deplore the violence but sympathize with the reasons for the violence"—which is equivalent to saying, "Of course we raped your women, dehumanized your men, and ghettoized the minds of your children, and you have a right to be upset, but that is no reason for you to burn our buildings. If you people keep acting like that, we will never give you your freedom."

I. Toward Liberation

Christians, unfortunately, are not known for their revolutionary actions. For the most part, the chief exponents of the Christian tradition have been identified primarily with the structures of power and only secondarily with the victims of power. This perhaps explains why white Christians in America tend to think of "love" as an absence of power and "reconciliation" as being indifferent to justice. It certainly accounts for the inauspicious distinction made between violence and force: "The state is invested with force; it is an organism instituted and ordained by God, and remains such even when it is unjust; even its harshest acts are not the same thing as the angry or brutal deed of the individual. The individual surrenders his passions, he commits violence."[9]

True, not all Christians have defended this perspective. The left wing tradition of the Protestant Reformation and the Quakers' stand on American slavery are possible exceptions. Prominent examples in our century are Reinhold Niebuhr's *Moral Man and Immoral Society,* the Confessing Church in Hitler's Germany, and particularly the noble example of Dietrich Bonhoeffer. We have already mentioned Jürgen Moltmann, and we could name other European theologians who are participating in the Marxist-Christian dialogue,[10] relating theology to

[9] Jacques Ellul, *Violence,* tr. C. G. King (New York: Seabury, 1969), p. 3. Ellul is not defending this viewpoint; he is explicating it.
[10] For an account of this dialogue, see Thomas Ogletree (ed.), *Opening for Marxist-Christian Dialogue* (Nashville: Abingdon, 1968).

revolutionary change. In America, Richard Shaull and Paul Lehmann have been defining the theological task according to the "politics of God," emphasizing the divine participation in the "messianic movements dedicated to the liberation of man from all that enslaves and dehumanizes him." [11]

But these examples are exceptions and not the rule. In America, at least, the Christian tradition is identified with the structures of racism in their oppression of black people. This was the reason for the white church's compliance with black slavery, its subsequent indifference toward oppression generally, and its failure to respond to the authentic demands of black reparations. No white theologian has taken the oppression of black people as a point of departure for analyzing the meaning of the gospel today. Apparently white theologians see no connection between blackness and the gospel of Jesus Christ. Even the so-called white American "theologians of revolution" did not receive their motivation from an identification with black Americans but from Latin America, Vietnam, and other foreign lands. I do not want to minimize their theological endeavors or question the authenticity of their verbalized identification with the poor, "undeveloped" nations, but I believe, as Sartre puts it: "The only way of helping the enslaved out there is to take sides with those who are here."

What then is the answer to the question, "What relevance has Christian theology to the oppressed blacks of America?" Since whites have ignored this question, it is necessary to look beyond the white Christian tradition to the biblical tradition, investigating the latter in the light of the past and present manifestations of the black struggle for liberation.

Taking seriously the tradition of the Old and New Testaments and the past and present black revolution in America, *black* theology contends that the content of Christian theology is *liberation*. This means that theology is a rational and passionate study of the revolutionary activity of God in the world in the light of the historical situation of an oppressed community, relating the forces of liberation to the essence of the gospel, which is Jesus Christ. Theology so defined moves us in the direction of the biblical tradition which focuses on the activity of God in history, liberating people from human bondage. God, according to the Bible, is known by what he does, and what he does is always related to the liberation of the

[11] See particularly Lehmann's *Ethics in a Christian Context* (New York: Harper, 1963) and *Ideology and Incarnation* (Geneva: John Knox Association, 1962).

oppressed. This is the meaning of the saying:

> You have seen what I did to the Egyptians, and how I bore you on eagles' wings and brought you to myself. Now therefore, if you will obey my voice and keep my covenant, you shall be my own possession among all peoples . . . (Exod. 19:45a, RSV).

Here the Exodus is connected with the covenant, revealing that Israel's consciousness as the people of God is bound up with the escape from Egyptian slavery. Yahweh is the God of the oppressed and downtrodden, and his revelation is made known *only* through the liberation of the oppressed. The covenant at Sinai, then, is not just a pious experience of God; it is a celebration of the God of liberation whose will is revealed in the freedom of slaves.

The equation of God's salvation with human liberation is found throughout biblical history, and particularly in God's incarnate appearance in Jesus Christ. By becoming the Oppressed One, God "made plain by this action that poverty, hunger, and sickness rob people of all dignity and that the Kingdom of God will fill them bodily with riches. The kingdom which Jesus preached and represented through his life is not only the soul's bliss but *shalom* for the body as well, peace on earth and liberation of the creature from the past."[12] This is the meaning of his birth in the stable at Bethlehem, his baptism with sinners, and his definition of his ministry for the poor, not the rich. God came to those who had no rights and "he celebrated the eschatological banquet."

> His resurrection from the humiliation of the cross can be understood as the revelation of the new creation of God's righteousness. In view of this, Christians are commissioned to bring . . . the justice of God and freedom into the world of oppression.[13]

With liberation as the essence of the Christian gospel, it becomes impossible to speak of the God of Hebrew history, the God who revealed himself in Jesus Christ, without recognizing that he is the God *of* and *for* those who labor and are heavy laden.

The emphasis on liberation not only leads us to the heart of the biblical message, it also enables theology to say something relevant to the black revolution in America. The liberation theme relates black power to the Christian gospel, and renders as an untruth the unverbalized white assumption that Christ is white, or that being Chris-

---

[12] Moltmann, *op. cit.*, p. 103.
[13] *Ibid.*, pp. 104–105.

tian means that black people ought to turn the other cheek—as if we blacks have no moral right to defend ourselves from the encroachments of white people. To explicate the meaning of God's activity as revealed in the liberation of the oppressed blacks of America means that the theologian must lose his identity with the white structure and become unqualifiedly identified with the wretched of this land. It means that there can be no authentic Christian talk unless it focuses on the empowerment of the poor—defined and limited by their past, present, and future history. If God is truly the God of the weak and helpless, then we must critically reevaluate the history of theology in America, a theology that owes more to white oppressors than oppressed blacks or Indians. What about Gabriel Prosser, Denmark Vesey, and Nat Turner as theological sources for assessing the contemporary presence of Christ? Could it be that American theologians can best understand their task by studying LeRoi Jones, Malcolm X, or the Black Panthers rather than merely mouthing the recent rhetoric of German theologians? Hopefully, the rise of black theology will force American religionists to realize that no theology of the Christian gospel is possible which ignores the reality of the divine among black people in this country.

II. Violence As Curse and As Right

The black revolution involves a total break with the white past, "the overturning of relationships, the transformation of life, and then a reconstruction."[14] Theologically, this means that black people are prepared to live according to God's eschatological future as defined by the present reality of the black kingdom in the lives of oppressed people struggling for historical liberation. It is this perspective that informs black theology's reflections on the religious significance of the black revolution in America.

Because the black revolution means a radical break with the existing political and social structure and a redefinition of black life along the lines of black liberation, it is to be expected that white Christians and assorted moralists will ask questions about methods and means. Theologically and philosophically, they want to know whether revolutionary violence can be justified as an appropriate means for the attainment of black liberation. If black theology is

[14] Vitaly Baroxoj, "Why the Gospels are Revolutionary: The Foundation of a Theology in the Service of Social Revolutions" in IDO-C (ed.), *When All Else Fails* (Philadelphia: Pilgrim, 1970).

Christian theology, how does it reconcile violence with Jesus' emphasis on love and reconciliation? Is it not true that violence is a negation of the gospel of Jesus Christ?

These are favorite *white* questions, and it is significant that they are almost always addressed to the oppressed and almost never to the oppressors. This fact alone provides the clue to the motive behind the questions. White people are not really concerned about violence *per se* but only when they are the victims. As long as blacks are beaten and shot, they are strangely silent, as if they are unaware of the inhumanity committed against the black community. Why did we not hear from the "non-violent Christians" when black people were *violently* enslaved, *violently* lynched, and *violently* ghettoized in the name of freedom and democracy? When I hear questions about violence and love coming from the children of slave masters whose identity with Jesus extends no further than that weekly Sunday service, then I can understand why many black brothers and sisters say that Christianity is the white man's religion, and that it must be destroyed along with white oppressors. What white people fail to realize is that their questions about violence and reconciliation are not only very naive, but are hypocritical and insulting. When whites ask me, "Are you for violence?", my rejoinder is: "Whose violence? Richard Nixon's or his victims'? The Mississippi State Police or the students at Jackson State? The Chicago Police or Fred Hampton? What the hell are you talking about?" If we are going to raise the question of violence, it ought to be placed in its proper perspective.

(1) Violence is not only what black people do to white people as victims seek to change the structure of their existence; violence is what white people *did* when they created a society for white people only, and what they *do* in order to maintain it. Violence in America did not begin with the black power movement or with the Black Panther Party. Contrary to popular opinion, violence has a long history in America. This country was born in violent revolution (remember 1776?), and it has been sustained by the violent extermination of red people and the violent enslavement of black people. This is what Rap Brown had in mind when he said that "violence is American as cherry pie."

White people have a distorted conception of the meaning of violence. They like to think of violence as breaking the laws of their society, but that is a narrow and racist understanding of reality. There is a more deadly form of violence, and it is camouflaged in such slogans as "law and order," "freedom and democracy," and "the American way of life." I am speaking of white collar violence, the violence of Christian murderers and patriot citizens who define right in terms of whiteness and wrong as blackness. These are the people who hire assassins to do their dirty work while they piously congratulate themselves for being "good" and "nonviolent."

I contend, therefore, that the problem of violence is not the problem of a few black revolutionaries but the problem of a whole social structure which outwardly appears to be ordered and respectable but inwardly is "ridden by psychopathic obsessions and delusions"[15] —racism and hate. Violence is embedded in American law, and it is blessed by the keepers of moral sanctity. This is the core of the problem of violence, and it will not be solved by romanticizing American history, pretending that Hiroshima, Nagasaki, and Vietnam are the first American crimes against humanity. If we take seriously the idea of human dignity, then we know that the annihilation of Indians, the enslavement of blacks, and the making of heroes out of slaveholders, like George Washington and Thomas Jefferson, were America's first crimes against humankind. And it does not help the matter at all to attribute black slavery to economic necessity or an accident of history. America is an unjust society and black people have known that for a long time.

(2) If violence is not just a question for the oppressed but *primarily* for the oppressors, then it is obvious that the distinction between violence and nonviolence is false and misleading. "The problem of violence and nonviolence is an illusory problem. There is only the question of the justified and unjustified use of force and the question of whether the means are proportionate to the ends";[16] and the only people who can answer that problem are the victims of injustice.

Concretely, ours is a situation in which the only option we have is that of whites or blacks. Either we side with oppressed blacks and other unwanted minorities as they try to redefine the meaning of their existence in a dehumanized society, or we take a stand with the American government, whose interests have been expressed in police clubs and night sticks, tear gas and machine guns. There is no possibility of neutrality—the moral luxury of being on neither side.

[15] Thomas Merton, *Faith and Violence* (Notre Dame: Notre Dame U.P., 1968), p. 3.
[16] Moltmann, *op. cit.*, p. 143.

Neither the government nor black people will allow that. The government demands support through taxes, the draft, and public allegiance to the American flag. Black people demand that you deny whiteness as an appropriate form of human existence, and that you be willing to take the risk to create a new humanity. With Franz Fanon, we do not believe it wise to leave our destiny to Europeans. "We must invent and we must make discoveries. . . . For Europe, for ourselves, and for humanity . . . we must turn over a new leaf, we must work out new concepts, and try to set afoot a new man."[17]

(3) If violence versus nonviolence is not the issue but rather the creation of a new humanity is, then the critical question for Christians is not whether Jesus committed violence or whether violence is theoretically consistent with love and reconciliation. The question is not what Jesus *did,* as if his behavior in the first century is the infallible ethical guide for our actions today. We must ask not what he did but what he is *doing,* and what he did becomes important only insofar as it points to his activity today. To use the Jesus of history as an absolute ethical guide for people today is to become enslaved to the past, foreclosing God's eschatological future and its judgment on the present. It removes the element of risk in ethical decisions and its judgment on the present. It removes the element of risk in ethical decisions and makes people slaves to principles. But the gospel of "Jesus means freedom"[18] (as Ernst Kasemann has put it), and one essential element of that freedom is the existential burden of making decisions about human liberation without being completely sure what Jesus did or would do. This is the risk of faith.

My difficulty with white theologians is their use of Jesus' so-called "non-violent" attitude in the gospels as the primary evidence that black people ought to be nonviolent today. Not only have Rudolf Bultmann and other form critics demonstrated that there are historical difficulties in the attempt to move behind the kerygmatic preaching of the early church to the real Jesus of Nazareth, but, moreover, the resurrected Christ is not bound by first-century possibilities. Therefore it is possible to conclude that the man from Nazareth was not a revolutionary zealot, and still contend that the risen Christ is involved in the black revolution today. Though the Jesus of yesterday is important for our ethical decisions today, we must be careful where we locate that importance. It is not to be found in following in his

[17]   *The Wretched of the Earth* (New York: Grove Press, 1965), p. 255.
[18]   *Jesus Means Freedom*, tr. Frank Clarke (London: SCM Press, 1969).

steps, slavishly imitating his behavior in Palestine. Rather we must regard his past activity as a *pointer* to what he is doing now. It is not so much what he did, but his actions were signs of God's eschatological future and his will to liberate all people from slavery and oppression. To be for Jesus means being for the oppressed and unwanted in human society.

As Christians, we are commanded not to follow principles but to discover the will of God in a troubled and dehumanized world. Concretely, we must decide not between good and evil or right and wrong, but between the oppressors and the oppressed, whites and blacks. We must ask and answer the question, "Whose actions are consistent with God's work in history?" Either we believe that God's will is revealed in the status quo of America or in the actions of those who seek to change it.

Accepting the risk of faith and the ethical burden of making decisions about life and death without an infallible guide, black theology contends that God is found among the poor, the wretched, and the sick. "God chose what is foolish in the world to shame the wise [wrote Paul], God chose what is weak in the world to shame the strong, God chose what is low and despised in the world, even the things that are not, to bring to nothing things that are. . ." (1 Cor. 1:26f.). That was why God elected Israelite slaves and not Egyptian slavemasters—the weak and the poor in Israel, not the oppressors. As Jesus' earthly life demonstrated, the God of Israel is a God whose will is made known through his identification with the oppressed and whose activity is always identical with those who strive for a liberated freedom.

If this message means anything for our times, it means that God's revelation is found in black liberation. God has chosen what is black in America to shame the whites. In a society where white is equated with good and black is defined as bad, humanity and divinity mean an unqualified identification with blackness. The divine election of the oppressed means that black people are given the power of judgment over the high and mighty whites.

III. Two Kinds of Reconciliation?

When black theology emphasizes the right of black people to defend themselves against those who seek to destroy them, it never fails that white people then ask, "What about the biblical doctrine of reconciliation?" Whites who ask that question should not be surprised if blacks

74

respond, "Yeah man, what about it?" The difficulty is not with the reconciliation question *per se* but with the people asking it. Like the question of violence, this question is almost always addressed *to* blacks *by* whites, as if we blacks are responsible for the demarcation of community on the basis of color. They who are responsible for the dividing walls of hostility, racism, and hate, want to know whether the victims are ready to forgive and forget—without changing the balance of power. They want to know whether we have any hard feelings toward them, whether we still love them, even though we are oppressed and brutalized by them. What can we say to people who insist on oppressing black people but get upset when black people reject them?

Because black liberation is the point of departure of black theology's analysis of the gospel of Jesus, it cannot accept a view of reconciliation based on white values. The Christian view of reconciliation has nothing to do with black people being nice to white people as if the gospel demands that we ignore their insults and their humiliating presence. It does not mean discussing with whites what it means to be black or going to white gatherings and displaying what whites call an understanding attitude—remaining cool and calm amid racists and bigots.

To understand the Christian view of reconciliation and its relation to black liberation, it is necessary to focus on the Bible. Here reconciliation is connected with divine liberation. According to the Bible, reconciliation is what God does for enslaved people who are unable to break the chains of slavery. To be reconciled is to be set free; it is to have the chains struck off the body and mind so that the creatures of God can be what they are. Reconciliation means that people cannot be human and God cannot be God unless the creatures of God are liberated from that which enslaves and is dehumanizing.

When Paul says, "God was in Christ reconciling the world unto himself," this is not a sentimental comment on race relations. The reconciling act of God in Christ is centered on the cross, and it reveals the extent that God is willing to go in order to set people free from slavery and oppression. The cross means that the Creator has taken upon himself all human pain and suffering, revealing that God cannot be unless oppression ceases to be. Through the death and resurrection of Christ, God places the oppressed in a new state of humanity, now free to live according to God's intentions for humanity.

Because God has set us free, we are now commanded to go and be reconciled with our neighbors, and particularly our white neighbors.

But this does not mean letting whites define the terms of reconciliation. It means participating in God's revolutionizing activity in the world, changing the political, economic, and social structures so that distinctions between rich and poor, oppressed and oppressors, are no longer a reality. To be reconciled with white people means destroying their oppressive power, reducing them to the human level and thereby putting them on equal footing with other humans. There can be no reconciliation with masters as long as they are masters, as long as men are in prison. There can be no communication between masters and slaves until masters no longer exist, are no longer present as masters. The Christian task is to rebel against all masters, destroying their pretensions to authority and ridiculing the symbols of power.

However, it must be remembered that oppressors never take kindly to those who question their authority. They do not like "thugs and bums," people who disregard their power, and they will try to silence them any way they can. But if we believe that our humanity transcends them and is not dependent on their goodwill, then we can fight against them even though it may mean death.

8. Toward a Spirituality of Liberation

DANIEL L. MIGLIORE

In his remarkable book *A Theology of Liberation*, Gustavo Gutierrez writes, "There is a great need for a spirituality of liberation" (p. 136).[1] This call to a new spirituality, though easily overlooked, is central in Gutierrez' work, and its significance reaches far beyond the Latin American situation to which it is primarily addressed. The possibility of a "spirituality of liberation" breaks through the deadening alternatives so familiar in churches everywhere: prayer or politics, transformation of individuals or transformation of social conditions, a personal interpretation or a political interpretation of the gospel. Like so much else in Gutierrez' book, the call to a spirituality of liberation especially challenges Christians in affluent countries to raise very disturbing questions about themselves and their church life. What sort of spirituality dominates the churches in North America? Could a spirituality of liberation ever take root in them? What would be the conditions of the rise of this new spirituality?

I. The Latin American Context

Before turning to these questions, we must be clear about the original context of Gutierrez' discussion of a spirituality of liberation. This phrase describes the particular experience of Latin American Christians who have begun to participate actively in the cause of full human liberation in their lands oppressed by poverty and disregard of elementary human rights. Precisely because of their involvement, these Christians find themselves in need not only of new theological understanding but of a new spirituality. While emphasizing that

---

[1] Gustavo Gutierrez, *A Theology of Liberation* (Maryknoll, N.Y.: Orbis Books, 1973). All page references in the text are to this volume.

Daniel L. Migliore is associate professor of theology at Princeton Theological Seminary, Princeton, New Jersey.

rigorous theological reflection on the struggle for liberation is indispensable, Gutierrez nevertheless insists that the construction of a new theological framework and the development of new theological categories are not enough. "We need a vital attitude, all embracing and synthesizing, informing the totality as well as every detail of our lives; we need a 'spirituality' " (p. 203).

The crisis of spirituality arises from the same condition which has caused the crisis of theology. Both have been estranged from praxis. Gutierrez points out that theology has in the past served two primary purposes: the cultivation of spiritual growth through meditation on the Bible (theology as wisdom) and the articulation of the rationality of the faith in relation to the various sciences (theology as rational knowledge). While considering these tasks of theology permanent, he argues that there is a third task which if taken seriously redefines the other two. The third task of theology is critical reflection on historical praxis. In the light of the Word of God and in the context of full involvement in the struggle against oppression, theology has the responsibility of reflecting critically on the efforts of people to become free and to take part in shaping their future. Only as such "critical reflection on historical praxis" can theology become truly a liberating factor, "a theology which does not stop with reflecting on the world, but rather tries to be part of the process through which the world is transformed" (p. 15).

Like theology, Christian spirituality has been damaged by its divorce from praxis. "A spirituality," Gutierrez says, "is a concrete manner, inspired by the Spirit, of living the Gospel" (p. 204). According to the Apostle Paul, "where the Spirit of the Lord is, freedom is there" (2 Cor. 3:17). A spirituality is therefore inseparable from the practice of liberation. If the Spirit of Christ sets people free, then the spiritual life is essentially an orientation toward "complete freedom, the freedom from everything that hinders us from fulfilling ourselves as [children of God], and the freedom to love and to enter into communion with God and with others" (p. 204). Traditional spirituality, estranged from the struggle against oppression in the world today, often fosters only "childish attitudes, routine, and escapes" (p. 136). Hence for many Christians in Latin America, "the participation in the process of liberation causes a wearying, anguished, long and unbearable dichotomy between their life of faith and their revolutionary commitment" (p. 135).[2]

[2] Cf. José Miguez Bonino, "Popular Piety in Latin America," in *The Mystical and Political Dimension of the Christian Faith*, ed. by Claude Geffré and Gustavo Gutierrez (New York: Herder and Herder, 1974).

Gutierrez contends that this dichotomy is false. The struggle for the liberation of human life in its political, social, and economic dimensions and the gift of liberation in Christ are not separate but interpenetrating processes. Their interpenetration requires that we both transcend every reductionism in understanding the liberation process and move toward a radically new kind of Christian spirituality.

On the one hand, the Christian life includes the social struggle. "The struggle for a just society is in its own right very much a part of salvation history" (p. 168). Rooted in the scriptural witness to the God who acts on behalf of the oppressed, a spirituality of liberation motivates participation in the cause of social justice. On the other hand, the struggle for freedom and justice needs the witness of Christian spirituality. While the creation of a just society is an historical task, its ultimate precondition is the gift of freedom in Christ. The experience of freedom as a gift, which is at the heart of a spirituality of liberation, points to a transcendent source of the liberation struggle and helps to keep this struggle open. Thus prayer and the celebration of the Supper of the Lord have political significance precisely in their "uselessness." As experiences of gratuitousness, they are sources of freedom in the midst of every effort, whether reactionary or revolutionary, to reduce human beings to things which are designated "useful" or "useless" (p. 206).[3]

Thus for Gutierrez the participation of Christians in the struggle for liberation is neither driven by dialectical theory nor aimed *solely* at the alteration of social and economic conditions. "The goal is not only better living conditions, a radical change of structures, a social revolution; it is much more: the continuous creation, never ending, of a new way to be human" (p. 32). This goal cannot be fulfilled apart from the grace of God which overcomes human sin and creates a new beginning of life in communion with God and others. "We are far from that naive optimism which denies the role of sin in the historical development of humanity" (p. 175).

Sin is, however, more than a private and interior reality; it has political dimensions and appears in oppressive and unjust social conditions. As selfish turning in on oneself and disregard of others, sin is the underlying cause of poverty, injustice, and exploitation. Recognition of sin as the root of human bondage does not minimize the importance of changing unjust institutions and societies, although it

---

[3] Cf. Segundo Galilea, "Liberation as an Encounter with Politics and Contemplation," in *The Mystical and Political Dimension of the Christian Faith*.

does make us aware that "a social transformation, no matter how radical it may be, does not automatically achieve the suppression of all evils" (p. 35). No human achievement should be confused with the realization of the kingdom of God.

Christian hope opens us, in an attitude of spiritual childhood, to the gift of the future promised by God. It keeps us from any confusion of the Kingdom with any one historical stage, from any idolatry toward unavoidably ambiguous human achievement, from any absolutizing of revolution. In this way hope makes us radically free to commit ourselves to social praxis, motivated by a liberating utopia and with the means which the scientific analysis of reality provides for us. And our hope not only frees us for this commitment; it simultaneously demands and judges it (p. 238).

Thus a Christian spirituality, developed in relation to liberating praxis, contributes to that praxis both motivation and a transcending dynamic. The new spirituality of liberation expresses and sustains commitment to the process of liberation in all of its dimensions. And such a spirituality constitutes a living witness in the midst of struggle that "the fullness of liberation—a free gift from Christ—is communion with God and with others" (p. 36).

It is in the life of "Christian poverty" that the spirituality of liberation concretely manifests itself. Gutierrez means by this phrase something quite different from a romantic or idealistic view of poverty. Christian poverty means "total availability to God" who became poor for our sake. It therefore involves solidarity with the poor and protest against material poverty. "Only by rejecting poverty and making itself poor in order to protest against it can the church preach something that is uniquely its own: 'spiritual poverty,' that is, the openness of human existence and history to the future promised by God" (pp. 302f.).

II. The Crisis of Spirituality

I am aware of the danger of asking how Gutierrez' call to a spirituality of liberation speaks to the churches in North America. It is all too easy for Christians in relatively affluent circumstances to co-opt, sloganize, and domesticate his proposals. Yet there is also the opposite danger of failing to ask the hard questions of the need and possibility of a new spirituality in our own situation. Hence an effort to examine ourselves in response to Gutierrez' reflections should not be avoided.

In the first place, the call to a spirituality of liberation makes us painfully aware of the crisis of spirituality in our own churches. We are compelled to acknowledge that concern for the spiritual life in our churches is either absent or assumes largely alienating forms. The existing expressions of Christian spirituality among us are almost entirely privatistic. They are narrowly focused on the salvation of the solitary soul rather than on the coming of God's kingdom. They are divorced from historical praxis. The self which is the center of these spiritualities is an asocial and ahistorical middle-class self. There is little awareness of the corporate and relational meanings of salvation, rebirth, and new creation as found in the biblical witness. To be in Christ is not to be set free to be a self in the privatistic sense; it is to be liberated for responsible participation in a new and inclusive community. Some forms of Christian spirituality seem to cut Christians off from rather than binding them ever more closely to wider circles of human need and hope.

A spirituality is the cultivation of full human freedom under the Spirit of Christ, a process of growing into mature personhood in Christ (Eph. 4:13). It is the discovery through Christ of new life in relationship with God and in solidarity with others. At its center has always been the venture of being united with Christ by faith, maturing into his likeness, participating in his death, and sharing in the power of his resurrection through prayer, meditation, hearing the Word, celebrating the sacraments, and serving others in his name. The spiritual pilgrimage is the loss of the old self-enclosed life for the sake of a new way of life in fellowship with God and with all his creatures.

Through the centuries different forms of Christian spirituality have arisen. Each has expressed a somewhat distinctive understanding of what it means to be united with the crucified Lord. Medieval piety included the devotional practice of the stations of the cross. Calvin described Christian life as self-denial and bearing the cross. Later pietists concentrated on the passion and wounds of Jesus. Each Christian spirituality, at its best, has aimed at the transformation of human life from self-preoccupation to a new corporate identity through the power of God's self-giving love in Jesus Christ.

For many Christians earlier expressions of spirituality have broken down completely. This breakdown is neither to be denied nor regretted. Nostalgia for the forms of piety we have lost only compounds our problem. In Gutierrez' words: "Not only is there a contemporary history and a contemporary Gospel; there is also a contemporary spiritual experience which cannot be overlooked. A spirituality means a reordering of the great axes of the Christian life in terms of this contemporary experience" (p. 204). Like other aspects of the life of the church, the spiritual life is a historical and changing reality. No less than doctrines or institutional structures, the spiritual life stands under the reforming authority of the Word of God as it addresses new situations. *Ecclesia semper reformanda* applies here as elsewhere.

The vacuum left by the breakdown of earlier forms of spirituality is being filled today by charismatic movements or by spiritual disciplines of the East. A critique of these movements is certainly legitimate to the extent that they focus on sensational phenomena, such as speaking in tongues, or confirm people in their apathy about social and political evils. But any critique of these movements would be blind if it failed to recognize the real crisis of spirituality in the churches. Many people at least dimly perceive the shallowness and meaninglessness of their life in a materialistic technological society. They want to experience genuine community. They long to be connected with a dynamic movement toward a significant goal. Their frantic search for their identity betrays their own need of liberation.

We need a new spirituality that can connect us with the agony and aspiration of other people. We need a spirituality that gives us a new sensitivity to the victims of oppression. Gutierrez is surely right: what we need is not less interest in the spiritual life but a transformation of it. We need a spirituality which is inclusive rather than exclusive, active as well as receptive, oriented to the changing of this world rather than its abandonment in favor of another world. We need a spirituality which connects our becoming free as persons to the entire historical process as a struggle for liberation. We need a spirituality of liberation which will open us increasingly to a life of solidarity with others, especially with the poor.

III. The Biblical Witness

If Christian life or spirituality is in a state of crisis in our churches, the basis and criterion of a new spirituality of liberation can be none other than the biblical witness read in relationship to actual struggles for liberation.

The event of Exodus from bondage in Egypt is decisive for the Old Testament understanding of God and the meaning of salvation. As Gutierrez writes: "The liberation of Israel is a political action. It is the breaking away from a situation of despoliation and misery and the beginning of the construction of a just and fraternal society" (p. 155). In the event of the Exodus, God manifested his concern for the oppressed and his will that they be free. When Israel was established as a nation, the prophets continually reminded the people of God's concern for the poor and the powerless and his inevitable judgment on those who live in luxury by cheating and neglecting the poor of the land.

Liberation as the goal of God's activity in history acquires still deeper meanings in the New Testament. Jesus called people to a new freedom in relation to God, teaching his disciples to address God as Father and proclaiming the forgiveness of sins. According to the gospel of Luke, Jesus defined his mission as the proclamation of freedom to those in bondage: "The Spirit of the Lord is upon me, because he has anointed me to preach good news to the poor. He has sent me to proclaim release to the captives and recovery of sight to the blind, to set at liberty those who are oppressed, to proclaim the acceptable year of the Lord" (Luke 4:18–19). Jesus shocked respectable people by having table fellowship with sinners and tax-collectors. He was partisan to the despised and poor people of his society. His message of the coming kingdom was directed especially to victims of injustice and poverty: "Blessed are you who are poor, for the kingdom of God is yours" (Luke 6:20).

Despite efforts of some scholars to prove otherwise, Jesus was not a Zealot, though a few of his disciples may have been attached to this revolutionary movement. Nevertheless, Jesus was crucified as a blasphemer and a disturber of society. The religious leaders and the Roman authorities combined to bring about his execution. The trial and crucifixion of Jesus had unmistakably political dimensions. Jesus died as a political criminal. This fact provides an important clue to the unity of his life and death. In his ministry and passion Jesus identified himself with the poor, the outcast and the victims of injustice. He was hanged between two thieves outside the gate. J. B. Metz is right, therefore, when he speaks of the memory of the passion story as a "dangerous memory." Memory of the crucified Jesus creates opposition to unjust social orders and a deep sense of solidarity with all who are oppressed and victimized.

In addition to the passion story itself, the Magnificat (Luke 1:46ff.) and the parable of the last judgment (Matt. 25:31ff.) powerfully express the solidarity of the Christ of God and his people with the oppressed of the earth. These are clearly crucial texts in the cultivation of a spirituality of liberation. As a hymn praising God for his gracious lifting up of the lowly, the Magnificat has radical social implications usually overlooked by traditional Catholic Marian piety and by the sentimental Protestant cult of mother and child. The parable of the last judgment is equally emphatic in its partisanship toward the poor. According to this parable, since Jesus has so fully identified himself with those in need, serving Jesus must take the form of concrete service to the hungry, thirsty, homeless, naked, sick, and imprisoned brothers and sisters of the crucified Lord.

That liberation in Christ brings a new awareness of human solidarity, and especially solidarity with the poor, is also the Pauline witness. The Christian life for Paul is life in union with Christ or life informed by his Spirit. This Spirit of Christ is the Spirit of freedom (2 Cor. 3:17). Christ sets us free, in the first place, from bondage to the law, guilt and the dominion of death. But the freedom for which Christ sets us free (Gal. 5:1) is freedom *for* service as well as freedom *from* sin. In so far as Christians participate in the freedom of the crucified Lord, theirs is a freedom to expend themselves for others, a freedom to enter into solidarity with the poor and needy. By his suffering and death Christ entered into solidarity with all the poor and weak of this world. Hence being in Christ means sharing in his voluntary identification with the poor.

Union with the crucified Lord is for Paul a personal relationship with political significance. Being "in Christ" and "in the Spirit" provide the basis of Christian identification with the poor. The christological hymn of Philippians 2:5ff. is employed by Paul to make the point that Christian life is Christomorphic, shaped by Christ's own identification with the servant condition and indeed with the abused and murdered servant. The Corinthians are exhorted by Paul to express their solidarity with the poor of Jerusalem just as the Lord Jesus became poor for their sake (2 Cor. 8:9). Thus for Paul life in the Spirit means freedom, and this freedom is expressed in advocacy of the cause of the poor.

New Testament spirituality is an ongoing process of participation in the reversal of the existing order by the life, death, and resurrection of Christ. The Lord becomes a servant, and the servant is exalted to sonship. The sinner is forgiven, and the judge takes his judgment on himself. The poor are called blessed, and the rich are warned of the coming judgment. Participation in this conflict-laden reversal process involves a daily dying and learning a new way to be human: the way of solidarity with the oppressed.

IV. The Components

The components of a spirituality of liberation will be no different from that of earlier Christian spiritualities: the Bible, prayer, meditation, fellowship around Word and sacrament, and exercise of the gifts of the Spirit; but in the new spirituality these components acquire new meanings and functions.

As we have seen, in a spirituality of liberation the Bible is read as the story of God's liberation of the poor and the oppressed and of man's partnership in this process.

Meditation becomes dangerous recollection and daring hope: the dangerous recollection of the cross of Christ which deepens our sensitivity to the cries of the victims of injustice, and the daring hope in and visions of the transformation of all things generated by the life, death, and resurrection of Jesus.

Prayer includes praise and gratitude to God but also expostulating with him, asking when the divine righteousness will be manifest on the earth, when children will no longer die of hunger, when innocent civilians will no longer be murdered in the name of some ideology.

Fellowship around Word and sacraments renews and clarifies freedom in Christ and offers an anticipation of the ultimate community of liberation symbolized as the kingdom of God.

The gifts of the Spirit refer to all those resources of critical analysis, imagination, and compassion which Christians and others are given to contribute to the unfinished task of human liberation in all of its dimensions.

The new spirituality of liberation is a political spirituality, but it is not the tailoring of Christian life to the measurements of particular political ideologies. To speak of a political spirituality is to say that Christian devotion and commitment are not restricted to a private zone of existence but are directed to the full realization of human life in a transformed world.

This shift of Christian spirituality—from preoccupation with the self to solidarity with the poor and the oppressed—necessarily involves repentance, new birth conversion, mortification, and commitment. In a spirituality of liberation the content of these traditional terms is enlarged and deepened in the Christian praxis of freedom in an unfree world.

Repentance involves not only repenting for my sins but also for the evils of my society, which expand the freedom of some by holding others in bondage. Repentance includes the resolve to work for the transformation of political and economic structures which bring prosperity to my society by exploiting the people of other lands.

Conversion means more than turning around in the area of private habits and activities. In its deepest sense conversion means turning away from self-centeredness and turning to the neighbor who is held in bondage by unjust conditions which I help to maintain.

Mortification is far more than killing off inordinate personal desires and eliminating petty vices. It means dying to a way of life, a life-style which informs our entire culture and is based on competition, achievement and the survival of the "fittest."

New birth signifies not only an event in personal history but also the beginning of a new corporate existence. Not only individuals but institutions and societies need to die to an old, dehumanizing way of life and experience rebirth.

Commitment refers neither to an abstract devotion to a docetic Christ nor to a repressive allegiance to a rigid moral or theological system. Christian commitment is trust in and loyalty to the crucified Christ whose emancipating Spirit guides the groaning creation toward the full realization of "the glorious liberty of the children of God" (Rom. 8:21).

V. Solidarity with the Poor

Since the pattern of Christian life follows that of God's activity in Christ, a spirituality of liberation can grow only in the praxis of solidarity with the poor.[4]

Gutierrez writes: "A spirituality of liberation will center on a conversion to the neighbor, the oppressed person, the exploited social class, the despised race, the dominated country. Our conversion to the Lord implies this conversion to the neighbor" (pp. 204f.).

This conversion process is radical and costly. It involves conflict with and a break from an old pattern of life, inclusive of its social, economic, political, and cultural dimensions. "We have to break with our mental categories, with the way we relate to others, with our way of identifying with the Lord, with our cultural milieu, with our social class, in other words, with all that can stand in the way of a real, profound solidarity with those who suffer, in the first place, from misery and injustice" (p. 205).

These are hard sayings for middle-class North American Christians. But they are perhaps no harder than the saying of Jesus that it is exceedingly difficult for the rich to enter into the kingdom of God (Matt. 19:24). How might we *begin* to respond to this call to the praxis of solidarity with the poor?

[4] Cf. Jürgen Moltmann, *Kirche in der Kraft des Geistes* (Munich: Chr. Kaiser, 1975), pp. 302–15.

A first step would be for us North American Christians to achieve a critical awareness not only of the plight of poor people but also of our complicity in policies which exploit them. To *listen* to and to take seriously the liberation theologians—black, Latin American, women—offers at least a chance for the growth of a new critical awareness of ourselves and of our society. We should not underestimate the resistance to this arduous act of listening which will be encountered in ourselves and in the churches of suburban America. The judgment which the liberation theologians render on the structures of political and economic power of which we are the beneficiaries is very severe. To recognize that the comfortable way of life to which we have become accustomed is built upon the poverty of others demands openness and honest self-examination as opposed to defensiveness and self-deception. Thus the simple readiness to listen already constitutes a step in the direction of a new solidarity. Prayer and meditation as acts of human openness to God will, if authentic, also open us to the needs of our neighbors in this elementary sense of listening long and hard to those who speak on behalf of the poor.

Second, we have to discover the reality of bondage and the yearning for liberation *in our own situation.* This means, negatively, that we should not encourage romantic ideas of white middle-class Christians leading the struggle for liberation in black communities or in Latin American countries. As Frederick Herzog has reminded us, the struggle for liberation begins at home: "Liberation theology will be learned first of all in prison, in the migrant camp, or a cotton field, in an Indian reservation or in the church that will not ordain a woman as minister."[5] The point is that talk of solidarity with the poor should not become mere rhetoric unrelated to concrete action. The poor and oppressed are not ideas but particular people. If solidarity with the poor is to be more than a mere idea or a patronizing gesture, it will *begin* in relation to particular poor people in our own society. Just as hearing God's Word and receiving the bread and wine discipline our attention to the particularity of grace in the Lord who became poor for our sake, so it disciplines us to attend to the particularity of our neighbors near and distant. If we are not engaged in the struggle of the poor near us, we are unlikely ever to have any meaningful solidarity with the poor in distant lands.

Third, solidarity with the poor is a meaningless phrase apart from an actual *transformation of our style of life,* as individuals and as a

---

[5] "Liberation Theology Begins at Home," *Christianity and Crisis,* XXXIV (May 13, 1974), 98.

community of faith. Affluent societies waste unconscionable amounts of natural resources in their frenzy of self-indulgence and in their dark fears which demand ever larger military machines to assuage. Christian churches in these societies have not given witness by the stewardship of their own resources, nor have Christians in their own way of life, to an evangelical simplicity of life-style. Only a way of life characterized by simplicity and service could be a real basis for solidarity with the poor and authentic protest against material poverty. As Gutierrez rightly insists, the call to Christian poverty should not be misunderstood as an idealization of material poverty. Christian poverty is really an openness to God who emptied himself freely for our salvation. Far from justifying material poverty, this authorizes our protest against it. A spirituality of liberation, based upon the liberating love of God, would find its outward expression in a disciplined life of simplicity and the readiness to risk ourselves in acts of love. It involves protest, in concert with the poor, against every way of life and social and economic system which enriches the few by impoverishing the many.

* * * * *

In summary, there is indeed "a great need for a spirituality of liberation" not only among Latin American Christians struggling against poverty and denial of human rights in their lands but also among Christians in the different situations of North America. The old forms of spiritual life are dead, and the new ones which have appeared in our churches are often more alienating than life-transforming.

A spirituality of liberation, rooted in the biblical story of God's gift of liberation in Jesus Christ, can spring up and grow only in a praxis of solidarity with the poor which "begins at home." The particular actions expressing this solidarity will be different according to the concrete situation.

If they are not to become mere slogans, the call to a spirituality of liberation and the praxis of solidarity with the poor will require costly changes of life-style for North American Christians and courage to protest against policies and systems which keep the poor in their poverty. In the face of powerful resistance to such changes, Christian hope is severely tested. Nevertheless, by the grace of that power beyond ourselves drawing us to cross and resurrection, the impossible may yet be possible.

9. The Liberation and Ministry of Women and Laity

MARGRETHE B. J. BROWN

The call for liberation—toward new communities of hope, justice, and the full exercise of all human rights for all members of these communities—comes from many different experiences of oppression. Out of Latin America come cries for political freedom from centuries of oppression; from North American racial minorities come cries for freedom from white dominion over bodies and cultures; and from Europe we see new theological themes, focusing on eschatology, in the political struggles of Christians facing Marxist-ruled environments. Into this scene enter Western women—and very vocally American women—with a cry for liberation that is often questioned, if not laughed at outright. Those who suffer under the lack of the basic human necessities of food, shelter, health, and education have no easy way of understanding what American middle-class women claim they need in order to be accepted as full human beings. What is immediately obvious to the peoples from the Third World is that we live in the midst of an affluence supported by economic and military structures which oppress them. The internal inhumanities of that system, under which women here are oppressed, are less obvious to the outsiders. In addition, many Western men also reject the cry of women for liberation, either because their concept of their own superiority is such that any optional interpretation of the human community is absolutely impossible for them, or because they fear that women's claims have a legitimacy which, if taken seriously, would make their own status questionable; and they are afraid or unable to face an open future.

There are obviously many ways in which the Third World struggle for liberation and the particular issues dealt with by Third World liberation theologians are not congruent with those of European and American women. The particulars of women's concerns cannot be immediately identified with those of the black Americans, expressed by James Cone, or of Latin Americans, expressed by Gustavo

Gutierrez. At the same time, the singular issue of liberation of women in the North Atlantic region is too narrow to be treated in isolation and it would be shortsighted to do so. For one thing European and American women are far too intricately bound into a system and a culture which would splinter totally if their liberation were to consist merely of a separation from that culture and its males. This fact must be dealt with theologically as a concern that affects males and females alike, primarily as partners in the same creation, secondarily as persons with different specific existential and political agendas, which must be balanced on the basis of a common theology and recognition of the historically separate treatments of the sexes within societies. Surely, the future of women must mean being extricated from bondage to an oppressive life-style in our society, but because of the nature of the creation of human life as male and female one must simultaneously consider the need for men too to be freed from this bondage. There is no possible separation of the life and history of the one from that of the other. In the second place, European and American women, because we are so inextricably bound into the systems of the Western world, are also part of that world as it represses persons of other races and cultures—with whom we nevertheless share some experience of oppression by the very same system.

This paper will comment on some particular experiences of North Atlantic women in the church which stimulate our participation in the broader call for liberation, and then give some comparative notes reflecting on several different corrective suggestions and trying to understand what the liberation of women within our own culture might offer these other approaches. Finally, we shall make some suggestions regarding the contribution that a full and liberated participation of women can make to the general ministry and witness of the church. It will become evident that the issue of the role of women in the church is similar in many ways to that of the laity of the church.

History has made it impossible for a woman to approach the issue of ministry in the church from any arena other than that of the general ministry; out of that the question of a special ministry or priesthood, separate and ordained, for one or another specific purpose and by whatever perceptions, may or may not be raised. The study of the ordained ministry today must include an awareness that for centuries the traditional exclusion of women from the exercise of ordained ministry meant bondage—the bondage of isolation from full participation in the church by all. It is from the viewpoint of a woman and a layperson (majority experiences in the church universal) that we shall look at general ministerial functions in and of the church. The ecclesiological ramifications clearly suggest the need for and meaning of liberation of the total ministry of the church—and its members as well.

Historically theology has been almost exclusively a male-originated discipline. Thus, it has not been fully human, though it has survived for centuries without the basic and radical challenge to expression of faith which now arises from the claims of liberation theologians and, among them, Western women. Within the home ground of the domineering theologies of the Christian churches (historically identified with the Western dominance) a claim is being made by women who have experienced an oppression more radically damaging than that by deprivation of food, shelter, health, or education, the oppression of being assigned secondariness in our very being as part of creation—within the *same* cultural framework that deprived the Third World of its material goods but could not steal its soul. Western women—at least those of the middle class or above—may have been fed, educated (within certain limitations), sheltered, and cared for by the best physicians in the world; but within the structures and rigidities of our societies the wholeness of our humanity and creativity has been as deprived as have the bodies of those who starve elsewhere. By being relegated to the primary and simplified structures of the nuclear family through the later centuries in which modern society has developed, woman has successfully been deprived of developing her full humanity, according to skill and insight, as a participant in and contributor to the complex society which is ours.

It may be that the real reason churches presently fail to meet the challenge of making any witness at a more complex level than that of the small rural communities and the isolated bedroom suburb is that they are tied to those places in society where they can pretend that simple structures of human life still persist. If women are locked out of the complex machinery of modern technological society, the church is there with them, well fed, well cared for, well sheltered—and even less aware of its fate. Some might think that is the right place for the church to be, with those disenfranchised from the complex systems of today's society. But when that is where the church remains, it is in the wrong place, for it has identified the bulk of its ministry as a ministry *to* them, rather than freeing and empowering them to participate in a general ministry to the world into which

Christians are called. The good news is not the news to "stay contentedly in your place," but rather to go to the ends of the earth and proclaim the gospel in witness throughout the complex systems of modern society. The church's call to identify with the marginalized does not mean it should stay there; it must hold before them the powerful hope of resurrection.

The problem of the exclusion of women from participating in the ministry of the church and the problem of the church's irrelevant structures for its total ministry to and in secular society are inextricably related. The church's placid acceptance of the marginalization of women in and by society is perhaps the most significant symptom of the illness which prevents it from presenting an honest witness to that society.

In that sense the issues of liberation for women, for minorities in the West, and for the people of the Third World are joint issues. The church too moved out along the colonizing route and maintained until this century an illegitimate control over the Christians it produced in other cultures. Only with the rise of secular freedom movements there were those Christians enabled to raise up their own churches and their own genuine structures of faith, through which witness might flow forth into their societies. Western churches had maintained "their children" as such rather than setting them free as disciples to carry out the proper extension of the witness by the first disciples, who did indeed grapple in a radical way with the issue of change and cultural differences in the formation of community life among the believers. Acts 2, 10, and 15 and Galatians 2 clearly indicate the experience of dealing with the issue of accepting or rejecting the mores of the local culture in particular situations.

The quest for liberation is thus related to the church's ability to witness at all, particularly to the women in our culture, who have become the symbols of the captivity of the church to its inverted life-style and its lack of the confidence with which the gospel must be proclaimed. Because it is a quest for liberation of the church as a whole, it is also a quest for liberation of people in the church in secular terms, as taxpayers, voters, soldiers—or conscientious objectors (a serious option of which women are deprived)—so that human life-styles may be set free according to the Creator's plan and not kept in captivity by other powers and principalities.

Obviously, the women of the West have been relieved of the labor of childbearing in the terms used by the early Hebrews to describe the separation of labor and punishment between the sexes (Gen. 3:16–

19). Western men have achieved parallel freedoms. Peoples of the Third World have not yet reached this point of convergence between demythologizing and technology. But although Western men have been released from toiling for bread, they still persist in ruling over both Western women, by excluding them from full participation in the fruits of their joint labor (both for bread and for children), and over non-North Atlantic people as a whole. The freedom achieved in Western society by technological means has been used to enslave those who do not have these means. Our gifts have been abused, and only a radical change in our communal patterns of living can be conducive to a genuine proclamation of the gospel. It is in this context that the specific issue of the place of women as part of the church's being and witness in the world must be worked at.

The issue of women's ministry, moreover, affects the role and continued place of the male—that is, ordained ministry within the churches' structures. As such, it is immediately threatening to those who have for so long lived as dominators, in the midst of bonds of human love and tied by its tensions to individual females as mothers, sisters, wives, and daughters. The challenge for such a reshaping of the human community causes chaotic reactions and radical resistance, individual as well as corporate, in the church, far more than the issues of self-determination and rights to means of production among Third World peoples, even though those issues also threaten the continuity of Western domination and thereby our present style of affluent living.

The issue of liberation of women (and the laity in general) for full participation in the church's whole ministry must not be cut short at the point of merely incorporating more women into the ranks of the clergy and the traditional decision-making processes of the church. The US Department of Labor may assume (Bulletin, June 1973) that women's search for work outside the home is based on economic reasons, but the church must always stand in judgment on the economic systems which surround it. The functions of the clergy and the decision-making processes of the church's life obviously do not aim at economic gain, though within a given economic system lifting oppression from a certain group may lead to their participation in the governance of the system and subsequent redistribution of economic gains.

The church must give much more thorough attention to those of its functions which it has grudgingly left for women (and laity) to perform. Take, for example, church school teaching and local community care. These bear marked resemblance to two facets of Calvin's fourfold ministry: teaching (by the doctors) and doing works of mercy (by the deacons). Again, we note the effects of the church's isolation within the marginalized communities of nuclear family structures in suburbia and in small rural towns: in places of higher learning and in government, where the same concerns of learning and community care are dealt with on behalf of our total society, both the church and women are notably absent.

It is one concern to incorporate women and Third World people into the traditional oppressive functions of the Western ruling class within the world community. But as far as long-term results and solutions to human problems are concerned, the harder task is overcoming the deprivation, within the ruling and decision-making processes of the world, of the skills, experiences, and insights of the oppressed. What is the significance in the understanding and functions of solidarity in tribal life, over against the pressures for individualized competition within Western male life; of emotional self-expression among black Americans over against the philosophy of the "stiff upper lip"; of service and nurture among women, over against the plundering of resources?

We shall now turn attention to some other approaches to theology which placed the call for liberation before us.

Ernst Bloch quotes Karl Marx:

> The social principles of Christianity preach cowardice, self-contempt, humiliation, humility, submissiveness—in short all qualities of the scum: and the proletariat that will not be treated as scum has far more need of courage, of self-confidence, of pride, and of a sense of independence than it has of bread. The social principles of Christianity are craven, and the proletariat is revolutionary.[1]

The church's identification with the world, at the point of sanctioning the oppression of women by society and of accepting and supporting the same principles within its own structures, is a witness to nothing else but the cravenness of the image of God as a dominant, blue-eyed, blond, wavy-haired, straight-nosed, sexy Aryan male. Although a woman, as any man, is tied by the similar bonds of love, not only corporately as a Westerner but also individually to a father, brother, husband, and son, she has to insist with Bloch that society must change and that the church must change—knowing that that is a

---

[1] Ernst Bloch, *Man on His Own* (New York: Herder and Herder, 1970), p. 138.

revolutionary demand affecting even those she loves most. Bloch says, "If the goals of a man fighting for higher wages do not include the disappearance of a society that compels him to fight for wages at all, he will not get far in his fight for wages either."[2] Similarly, the challenge of this paper is to gain acceptance for the otherness of human experience—exemplified here by sex, elsewhere by race, culture, nationality, language—and to enter into a common dialogue, honoring not only what has been the dominating experience, but also the experience of the oppressed, which may actually be intrinsically stronger simply because it survived in spite of evil (a quite different thing from surviving as a result of evil). Jürgen Moltmann has suggested that Christianity

> installed itself as the "crown of society" and its "saving center," and lost the disquieting, critical power of its eschatological hope. In place of what the Epistle to the Hebrews describes as an exodus from the fixed camp and the continuing city, there came the solemn entry into society of a religious transfiguration of the world.[3]

Those who have come to know the church's imprisonment by the world, in the freedom we have been given in faith, must likewise concretely raise the issue of a conversion of the very church that lost the critical power of its eschatological hope and became structured by the shapes of the world, incorporating the oppressive powers of the world's principalities into its own being.

In the last chapter of *Theology of Hope*, Moltmann raises the question of concrete forms of living the eschatological hope in modern society. Moltmann suggests a path ahead in terms of promise, for he is a teacher who lives his thought out of the experiences of the past manifestations of the church. The consequences of that promise are inevitably different for those who look from a viewpoint other than that of a white male Anglo-Saxon Protestant. Moltmann describes a process of emancipation leading to a society focused solely on need and labor.[4] Most obvious here, within the relegation of religion and culture[5] to the realm of playthings of inclination, is the relegation not only of parts and facets of what he considers valid criteria within human life, but of Western women, who are no longer needed and who are excluded from the labor market in its widest connotations.

[2] *Ibid.*, p. 203.
[3] Jürgen Moltmann, *The Theology of Hope* (New York: Harper and Row, 1967), p. 42.
[4] *Ibid.*, pp. 304–11.
[5] *Ibid.*, p. 310.

Women are even aware that they are hardly needed as child-bearers for more than very few years of increasingly longer lives, and even that is being threatened by replacement with test-tube babies. If the churches have felt themselves in suburban captivity, they have indeed been there with suburban women, in solitary confinement, participants only in the "plays" of society, not in its basic human structures and relationships.

The attempt to claim the salvation of "man's" humanity in the cultivation of "his" subjecthood, with vast spaces available for inward expansion,[6] again affirms the actual isolation of the wife/mother in the nuclear family, where she is bereft of broader human responsible relationships. She may partake in vast undertakings of free-wheeling and ineffectively maintained voluntary organizations, but she may not enter into the political life which might provide liaison with those others who suffer under the inhumanity of the modern industrial society. In each case, the suburban woman is as isolated and bereft as are the poor, who are exploited economically by society, while she is maintained as a thing by and in the structures of affluence. She may fulfil certain needs but is forced to remain outside the possibility of being an initiator and contributor within the broader human community.

Again, in an essay on the "Present Anthropological Problem"[7] Moltmann discusses the difference between a society of having and one of being. We must note that the marginalization of middle- and upper-class women from participation in the needs and labors of society relegates them into a role of merely *having*. Women's search for more significant participation in the total life of the church cannot be limited to the very real need for placing more ordained women in our pulpits and at our altars to preach the word and administer sacraments—receiving equal and proper professional salaries for it. It must include the struggle to incorporate into the fulness of the church the historical and contemporary identification with all others oppressed by false domination as well as the fulfilling experience for women (and most of the laity) of serving in ministry in direct daily encounters with the world. The Reformers reclaimed the necessity of the presence and participation of the laity for the celebration of the Eucharist. Similarly, the function of the church in mission and ministry to the world, locally and systemically, must be incorporated into

6 *Ibid.*, pp. 311–16.
7 Jürgen Moltmann, *Religion, Revolution and the Future* (New York: Scribners, 1969), pp. 55ff.

the vision of the wholeness of the church. Such a stance on the part of the churches, affirming human life as *being* in the world as over against that of *having,* would be more than revolutionary, it would be "pro-volutionary."[8] This clearly puts pressure on vast areas of the churches' visible life-styles, salaries, and modes of budgeting for its own education, upbuilding, and celebration. It also offers the churches an opportunity to reclaim a reservoir of uninvested human abilities in developing a responsible relationship with the needs of the world. In short, this means a reshaping which brings into a new whole these two sides—not only of the male and the female but also of clergy and the entire *laos.* The ministries traditionally performed by men, publicly honored and paid and supported by elaborate structures from apostolic succession to district superintendents, those of preaching the word, administering sacraments, and church administration, must be brought together with the ministries, equally biblical, so frequently maintained by females in the forms of the Christian education of the children (as in the present Sunday schools in the US) and the care and nurturing of the sick (those functions of the organized church for which the Roman Catholic Church allowed nuns to organize, as the only permissible female form of organizational life).

This will indeed demand a new church, shaped by the internal dynamics of the gospel heritage, facing a world which participates in our agenda-setting whenever it makes clear its needs. If we look only at the issue of the exclusion of women from clergy positions in the church, we are simply assimilating the quest for freedom of many former revolutions, and thereby achieving nothing but another liberty.[9] As Marx describes the realm of freedom as the realm of work,[10] it must be made clear that this insight into the nature of the humane and of human society must not be neglected by the church's reshaping for mission in a society which radically needs to regain its full humanity not only in *having* but also in *being.* In a society such as ours, where having tends to be seen as the measure of human success and where the rich woman nevertheless finds herself imprisoned from her own being by what she "has" and is marginalized from broader human activities, since she, along with other possessions, "belongs to" her husband, we must raise the question of where humanness has actually been maintained within our society as a whole: among the decision-makers, whose decisions make some of us into things, or

[8] *Ibid.,* p. 32.
[9] *Ibid.,* p. 77.
[10] *Ibid.,* p. 75.

97

among the "things," who have been kept from participation in such inhuman decisions. The new future cannot be shaped without full consideration of the latter option as well.

The radical cry for incorporating women and laity into a genuine new being of the church is a call for participation in dialogue, not for a cautious exchange of balances of proven powers. It requires an examination of the common heritage of ministry, in which Christ is not only identified in the breaking of the bread and where two or three are together in prayer, but also when he heals the sick and makes the blind see. It is also a call for a radically new encounter with those who have not heard the gospel, but merely see the weaknesses of the churches' excessive and lopsided visible organization which has supported the marginalization of some of its own baptized members and condoned similar practices in society. The church cannot continue to disregard the fruits of the Spirit merely as desirable attributes of women (Gal. 5:22–23) and use them to "keep some in their place" rather than to move out and share. The church organized the gifts of the Spirit, clung to by the male priesthood, and was careful not to offer them any further away than where they could be controlled by the closed system upheld by the tradition of limited ordination and previously limited education. For the fruits of the Spirit are the descriptions of life in being, the gifts of Spirit as life in doing, and the separation or dominion of one over the other simply prevents the encounter of the Spirit with the world.

On the basis of this discussion of liberation and the pressure it exerts on traditional concepts of ecclesiology and the ordained ministry, we shall turn to the American liberation theologian James Cone, who in his book *A Black Theology of Liberation*[11] attempts to deal with a pressing and concrete situation in which the gospel of liberation must be allowed to function, that of the black Americans. Cone's approach, both here and in his earlier volume *Black Power and Black Theology,*[12] is refreshing on American ground because he attempts to deal with theology within a concrete situation, rather than as an abstract derivation from European thinking, a method which characterized much of American theological work previously.

Cone accuses American theology of being "white" and concerned only with the interests of the oppressors,[13] because it failed to relate

[11] Philadelphia: Lippincott, 1970.
[12] New York: Seabury, 1969.
[13] Cone, *A Black Theology of Liberation*, p. 22.

the gospel to the pain of the black experience. It might be more accurate to say that the failure of American theology was that it failed altogether to relate to the development of America as a community of human lives. Caught in individualistic pietism, a fact recognized also by Jürgen Moltmann, it allowed the formation of a nation to which it simply never addressed itself. Out of the history of migration from Europe, in order to gain religious freedom, only isolated "religious" communities developed. Out of the fear of repression due to the exercise of faith, faith appears to have been chased into the inner corners of separate lives, where it hibernated until American blacks—along with their African forebears—only recently seriously challenged our nonfunctional and nearly nonexistent ecclesiologies within the Protestant arena of life. Given the constant expansion of the American nation, controlled by a vision of unlimited growth in all facets of secular life, first moving westward and next out in domination of the Third World in neo-colonialism, it seems as if not one single separated and mystically pious individual ever even thought of relating himself as accountable to his brothers—let alone his sisters in the total American community—be they black or white. A nation which understood human life as a demand for expansion and for *having,* a nation in which slavery and the cultural ostracism of women were permitted, excluded both blacks and women from direct participation in the achievement of its expansion. Both groups were kept for use by the dominant group, the slaves for labor and the women for "home" work, breeding, and sexual entertainment. Since the latter pursuits required greater proximity to the oppressed group, the women benefited by receiving better food and shelter and eventually education, though the slaves gained the right to vote first. Both groups were kept out of the society of achievers and decision-makers who conquered this continent and beyond.

The failure of American theology, through privatization and individualization, bears some resemblance to the failure of pre-Reformation theology. Through an emphasis on the priest only as the instrument and purveyor of salvation, the pre-Reformation church lost the concept of the community of believers as the basis for the manifestation of the gospel, and its proclamation thus lost ecclesial creativity. Black theology, by contrast, arises out of a communal experience, forced as it may be, and therefore bears a valid claim to an ecclesial manifestation coordinate with its christological center. The corrective it properly addresses to the "white" theology which has pervaded the American scene is therefore not primarily or only that it

99

must become black or liberated or that it must emerge from an oppressed society. It must take seriously the Christology it espouses and verbalizes and the totality of the human experience to which its proclamation relates. The peculiar identity of the ecclesial community arises precisely through . its communal effort to theologize, not through an individualistic, romantic, pietistic description of something "other" felt by certain separate individuals.

What this demands is systemic change, not the exchange of black for white, not switching sides by oppressor and oppressed, each continuing the denial of the humanity of the other. Understandably in the present historical situation, Cone focuses only on the problem of oppression[14] rather than on the more radical cause of community *vs.* isolationism and alienation. Still, it behooves women to join their call for systemic change to that of the blacks, careful not to fall for the temptation to join latent racism among us to the fears of the past of dominance by men only. In this joint struggle, it is obvious that we must listen more closely to the voices of our black sisters.

Cone's view of black theology as survival theology is, however, too shallow. Not only is it anti-ecclesiastical, which is understandable and proper in view of the historical situation and the heritage of slavery, but it also appears to abrogate the reality of suffering as inevitable in Christian life by identifying injustice with suffering. A stronger relationship to the acclaimed christological bases of black theology might have prevented this. The question is not "to be or not to be,"[15] for in the light of the events of crucifixion and resurrection, "being" is given *a priori.* The beautiful Shakespearian formulation is nothing but another romantic dream, as Moltmann refers to the heresies of the nineteenth century.[16] The Christian faith unavoidably must challenge Camus's rebel, not at the point of his revolt but at the point of his fatalistic base, which is without hope for a common and communal future. The promise of the resurrection not only gives courage to rebel, but also indicates the hope of a victory which is primarily that of Christ, and therefore secondarily—in and through the body of Christ—a victory for humankind.

The problem continues throughout Cone's discussion of norms and sources for his theology. It is the same dichotomizing of human experience, first maintained by the oppressors, and then continued by the oppressed, who limit their expectation to the political arena,

---

[14]   *Ibid.*
[15]   *Ibid.*, p. 36.
[16]   *Ibid.*, p. 44.

which is determined by the oppressors, who only "have" but cannot be said to "be." Unfortunately, Cone does not here incorporate and utilize the precious black experience in the strong eschatological tenor of the Spirituals[17] of earlier centuries of survival. In his discussion of Barth, Tillich, and Bonhoeffer, Cone seems to forget that it was precisely from within the situation of the oppressed that Bonhoeffer said, "When Christ calls a man, he bids him to come and die."[18] No matter how much the biblical experience of the expectation of an immediate Second Coming of Christ has led later generations astray by not taking courage from that affirmation, it is nevertheless genuine. The Christian gospel does offer an authentic response to the experience of inhumanity through the assurance of God's participation—not necessarily always against[19]—but definitely always with and through human suffering, as Christ made evident on the cross and confirmed in the resurrection and the ascension.

Cone's discussion of God likewise falls short of the radical issue raised by God's insertion of himself into human history. The discussion of "whose god"—whether God is white or black—is inappropriate because the subject is wrong. The choice was, is and will be God's *to be for* humankind, out of his power, not ours, whoever we are or may pretend to be. God did choose to liberate the Israelites, but he also chose to let the Mesopotamians rule for a rather longish period of life-experience of the same Israelites. God is not only the God of black history, for better and for worse; he is also the God of all history, including that of the oppressors. To talk about God as that which is Wholly Other than the specificity of whiteness is to impose on God a limitation that is illegitimate within the knowledge of the forgiveness wrought in Jesus Christ for all people.

The challenge to conversion does not come in terms of black *or* white, in terms of the known and experienced categories of the past, regardless of the unjust suffering they include. It is a challenge to a conversion towards an unknown future in terms of the eschatological hope which gives "courage, self-confidence, pride and a sense of independence"—beyond the dependent relationships between oppressor and oppressed. Cone's serious reference to Moltmann unfortunately comes too late in his treatment of liberation,[20] and thereby misses the transformation of life, in faith, into a nonexclusive commu-

[17] Cf. Cone, *The Spirituals and the Blues* (New York: Seabury, 1972).
[18] Cone, *A Black Theology of Liberation*, p. 61.
[19] *Ibid.*, p. 84.
[20] *Ibid.*, pp. 244ff.

nity guided by such faith. He fails to inform the white society of its full apostasy in its refusal to live as a community at any level but the narrowest one of the nuclear family, in which we have allowed our technological society to imprison interhuman responsibility and accountability in relationships of love. Within the nuclear family structure there is little difference in the role of men, whether they are loosely attached through poverty and open sexual liberty to the mothers and children in the ghettoes or whether the lack of reliable relationship to men is felt through the reverse side of their successful engagement in the business of the technological society and the covert sexual liberty exercised through wife-swapping or relationship to call girls as practiced among affluent dwellers in suburbia. In either case, they are isolated from meaningful human relationships of mutual accountability to a variety of other persons and cast out to fight in lonely competition with their peers. Meanwhile, the mature women are imprisoned with their children away from decision-making processes and systems. Into this dichotomization of humanity that society maintains the proclamation of the gospel must be introduced to make whole the fragmented experience of human life. Liberation of women cannot mean merely the extension of their secular "rights" to behave according to the life-styles prevalent among the men. Liberation of women incorporates a call for the authentic restoration of the fulness of human community, not only bringing them out of the isolation of the nuclear family but freeing the men from the isolation and lonely alienation of the technological society focused on *having* and forced into roles of domination which destroy even the possibility of genuine human encounters.

Moltmann's theology portrays the biblical hope and suggests its meaning for the church, without suggestions for the actual needs of the church's life as such. Cone takes possession of the revelatory message that God creates a community, and without hesitation claims this creation of the church as belonging to the oppressed and the black, thereby cutting short its ultimate pronouncement of God's sovereignty over all of nature and history *vis-à-vis* the powers and principalities. From the Latin American struggle for liberation comes, in Gutierrez' book *A Theology of Liberation*, a plea for the whole church to be the carrier of liberation precisely because it is the sacrament of history.[21] As such, this may be the form of liberation

---

[21] Gustavo Gutierrez, *A Theology of Liberation* (Maryknoll, N.Y.: Orbis, 1973), pp. 255ff.

theology which has the most in common with the concern of this paper for the liberation of the whole ministry of the church.

Gutierrez defines the place for theological reflection

> ...as the understanding of the believer that arises spontaneously and inevitably in those who have accepted the gift of the Word of God. Theology is intrinsic to a life of faith seeking to be authentic and complete ... [it] is a pre-understanding of faith which is manifested in life, action, and concrete attitude.[22]

Theology is not merely wisdom or rational knowledge but the critical reflection on praxis. The privileged *locus theologicus* is the life, preaching, and historical commitment of the church. It thus becomes a liberating transformation of the history of humankind, and also therefore that part of humankind gathered into the *ecclesia* which openly confesses Christ.[23] By maintaining a relationship to the totality of history, in spite of the problems of the structures and life-styles of the church, Gutierrez avoids the problem of separatism and isolationism that eventually awaits Cone's black church and will inevitably turn it "white" in Cone's own terms. Gutierrez also avoids Cone's problem with God's exclusivity as black:

> In the sacrament the salvific plan is fulfilled and revealed; that is, it is made present among men for men. But at the same time, it is through the sacrament that men encounter God. This is an encounter *in* history, not because God comes *from* history, but because history comes from God. The sacrament is thus efficacious revelation of the call to communion with God and to the unity of all mankind. . . . The church is also provisional. . . . The break with an unjust social order and the search for new ecclesial structure . . . in which the most dynamic sectors of the Christian community are engaged . . . have their basis in this ecclesiological perspective. We are moving towards forms of presence and structure of the church the radical newness of which can barely be discerned on the basis of our present experience; . . . it has its root in the profound fidelity to the church as sacrament of the unity and salvation of mankind and in the conviction that its only support should be the Word which liberates. . . . The point is not to survive, but to serve.[24]

If the church is to be the church continuously, it must accept this challenge for radical newness within itself. It cannot remain simply in judgment on those outside itself, refusing the proclamation of the

[22] *Ibid.*, p. 3.
[23] *Ibid.*, pp. 12–15.
[24] *Ibid.*, pp. 259, 261f.; cf. Cone, *A Black Theology of Liberation*, p. 36.

gospel to them, while it continues to practice the same forms of apostasy by oppression and marginalization of some of its members, be they non-European, non-American, black, female, old, young. The ecclesial community is not only one centered around the union, in the eucharist, with the Father; it is also the unity of those who share in common ownership the goods necessary for earthly existence in a ministry to the world.[25]

From here Gutierrez moves to a discussion of poverty, material and spiritual. Material poverty is the root cause of a collective poverty that maintains the marginalization of the poor in a stable but unjust society.[26] As such, material poverty is scandalous. Equally so is spiritual poverty, which masks attachments to goods which are not shared over against total openness to God. At this point one can understand the scorn of the oppressed masses in the Third World for the claims of Western women to liberation. For the Western woman is inextricably caught at this point: she is provided for with overwhelming riches in material goods, and thus stands as the prized show thing of the successful Western male. She stands at the apex of human depravity from the point of view of the poor of the Third World—or for that matter of Western minority poor. She exists in society merely as the focal point for the collection of material possessions and therefore as the extreme human antithesis to the sharing of goods and the creation in faith of human *koinonia*. Her being here in society is affirmed, not challenged, by her being in the church, where she is removed from the administration of the sacraments and full participation in the churches' total ministry. Not only is she removed behind a wall of earthly possessions, but she is also removed from the decision that that is her place—or, in more accurate human terms, her prison. By excluding women from its point of administration and systems control, by excluding them from ordination, which it has made its cornerstone, the church has merely emphasized and supported the evil of the world and thereby itself fallen pray to the evil of exclusivity which denies full humanity to some of its members.

That women have maintained enough human quality and Christian faith to remain capable of expressing hope in a future under the common lordship of Jesus Christ is no less a miracle than that the suffering poor of the earth still claim a right to be human over against the powers and principalities of economic exploitation.

The ability to live in spite of poverty, independent of material

[25] Gutierrez, *op. cit.*, p. 264.
[26] *Ibid.*, pp. 288ff.

goods and without want, is becoming a primary concern for the Western churches in their participation in development programs, where, however, the churches must maintain the rights of the Third World culture to remain as optional cultures, not merely different economic systems. Likewise, women must become free, not merely to participate in a system already proven sinful through oppressiveness toward all whom it can distinguish from itself. Women must bring back the experience of love that has been harbored, in spite of everything, in the nuclear family, barely consisting of more than one woman and a few children for a few years. The care for the needy of our society through the volunteer groups they have grudgingly been permitted to form, despite the ineffectiveness of these groups, has also provided an important place for the hibernation of works of mercy as a genuine part of the church.

If the church is to continue its claim to be the "visible sacrament of this saving unity" with God in history,[27] it must answer the call for radical reshaping. This call comes out of its own history and tradition, not only as the safeguard of word and sacrament, but also as the agent in history of the God who cares for those marginalized in and by society. It must respond to the call that comes from those who are marginalized around it, by it, and in the midst of it. It cannot maintain a structure built on only parts of its nature and of its self-knowledge gained in encounter with the world in history. It must dare to realize its own ability to move into the future with courage and independence toward the structures of the world, and honor those whom the world despises and excludes. Obviously, such a reshaping involves far more than merely incorporation of women, poor, oppressed, or laity into a social structure which is never more than partial anyway. It involves the long hard work of incorporation into its total life-style those fruits of the Spirit which determine its shape as recognizably different from that of the society within which it is called not to survive but to serve.

It will be a church recognizable not only in sacrament and orders, but also in its mission and ministry to the world. It will be a church recognizable not only in the breaking of the bread and gathering in prayer: but it will also identify and treasure the ability to encounter those in need with its ministry—the poor, the sick, the blind, the uneducated, the oppressed. It will be a church which does not coerce those who are recognizably different from "its own," but which dares

[27] *Ibid.*, p. 260.

trust its own dependence on God alone sufficiently to enter into a dialogue where it may shed light on those who are "others," rather than insist on their incorporation into itself. It will be known not only through its public appearance and the works of its clergy, but also through the functions of all its people as they live within the whole of creation. Not only will it incorporate those who are or who have been oppressed at various points in history into the ranks of those ministering word and sacrament and structures, it will also represent an open and full sharing of the risks of mission and ministry. Its structures, shapes, and patterns of operation will incur immediate change and have to remain dynamically flexible in encounter with the changing needs of history and cultures.

The program for such a fully liberated ministry of the church cannot be laid out in the computerized style of much contemporary mission of the church. From a Reformed perspective, Calvin's suggestion of four offices in the ministry: preaching, ruling, caring, teaching, may offer an historically recognizable image and call us to review the lopsided shape in which prejudice against women has left the church at the present. The two offices of the pastor and the ruling elder have, for centuries, been maintained and until recently held exclusively by men, and as such have dominated the shape and image of the church. The two other offices and their adjoining ministries, of the deacons caring for those in need and the teachers educating the next generation, have for some time been relegated to women in the local churches. The oppression of women has in turn prevented these ministries from fully developing as part of the church. And the women who have functioned in those arenas of ministry of the church have been prevented from participating in the broader life of the church. Through the church's absorption of the social custom of keeping women out of the public arena, it has doubly distorted its own witness to the society around it—by aping the prejudice and also by thereby misrepresenting itself.

The liberation of women, and therewith the liberation of much of what has become the realm of lay ministry of the church at this time in history, has a theological precedent in Calvin's radical reform of the church. In order to meet the exigencies of our time, this emerging new pattern must be allowed to blossom into the full participation of *all* the partners in the church's ministry. The first test of such a ministry will be the universal scope of the freedom from oppression it proclaims in its encounter with *all* of God's creation.

10. Towards an Indigenous Theology of the Cross

DOUGLAS J. HALL

This is an attempt to summarize certain conclusions to which I have been led over the past three or four years as a teacher of Christian theology. But not as a teacher of theology only—also as a human being, a resident of North America, and, perhaps most significantly of all, as a father of four children. Increasingly, I have only been able to address myself to the theological task as one for whom the future, which as Jürgen Moltmann has shown us is the particular focus of that task, has ceased to be theoretical and impersonal. Through my children the future has acquired eyes. Being a sinful man, I needed their eyes to awaken me to all the other eyes that look at us—that look in a special, penetrating way at our generation—out of that future. Because of the myriad eyes (sometimes they are disturbingly present right in my classroom) I have gradually been deprived of many of the answers that I received from the generations of Christians preceding mine. For several years I was able to transmit them, even to consider them my own, but they have become too small in relation to the pain that is present, largely unknown to itself, in the eyes of my children. Not a few of those of my generation who have become conscious of these eyes of the future have concluded that there is nothing, after all, in the tradition of Jerusalem—or of Athens!—big enough to meet the pain. I understand them well enough. But I look about in the ruins of our once proud Christian religion, and I ask whether, if not answers, there may not be at least a place to which to bring the questions: a place of which, as a father, I should not have to be ashamed before the scrutiny of my children's eyes.

Douglas J. Hall is Professor of Christian Theology, McGill University, Montreal, Ontario. This paper was originally written for and presented to the North American Area Theological Committee. A recension of it has been published in Interpretation, Vol. XXX, No. 2 (April 1976).

I. The Occasion

In a profound essay entitled "In Defence of North America," the Canadian political philosopher George C. Grant makes this critical observation about the character of North American theology:

> In a field as un-American as theology, the continually changing ripples of thought, by which the professionals hope to revive a dying faith, originate from some stone dropped by a European thinker.[1]

What is most distressing about this statement is its proximity to truth. There are obvious exceptions, yet the general character of theological thought on this continent has been consistently informed by European patterns and movements. The extent to which this is so has been underscored for some of us today by the emergence of a so-called black theology which explicitly rejects the European adherence. In an issue of *Christianity and Crisis,*[2] C. Eric Lincoln complained of the practice of sending theologians off to Europe for indoctrination: there, he said, they cannot find "light for *our* darkness."

Theology is by no means alone in this adherence to the mother culture. Like our intellectual traditions in general, it was shaped at first by the great wave of European expectancy on the crest of which this continent was established, namely that modernity which emerged into view in the sixteenth and seventeenth centuries. Although for obvious reasons theology came into closer contact with the indigenous culture of this continent than did other intellectual aspects of the civilization imported from Europe, it was not altered by that contact. On the contrary, it contributed in its own way to the annihilation of the cults and culture of the North American Indian. And throughout these few centuries, theology in North America has functioned primarily as a translation (usually into pragmatic terms) of reflections (usually more profound reflections) offered by European Christians.

It would not be entirely wrong to interpret this tendency as a dimension of the problem of authority which has existed for us as a people at many levels. The most decisive doctrinal emphases for the churches of the "New World" *did* emerge out of events, European events, which antedate our own history. And these emphases *have* been fostered by ecclesiastical ties, whether formal or informal, in which North American churches were usually the subordinate part-

[1] George Grant, *Technology and Empire: Perspectives on North America* (Toronto: House of Anansi, 1969), p. 16.
[2] C. Eric Lincoln, in *Christianity and Crisis,* XXX, No. 18 (Nov. 2–16, 1970), 226.

ners. Yet this is by no means a satisfactory explanation of the question. In fact, precisely because these *doctrinal* influences antedate the modern epoch embodied in the North American experiment, they are less symptomatic of the problem to which Grant alludes than is the more specifically *theological* phenomenon, namely, the tendency of North American theology to reflect the latest European trend—and to do so, incidentally, without much concern for the doctrinal "orthodoxy" established by earlier denominational influences.

While this adherence to Europe can be noted in many fields of human endeavor, including even the natural sciences, theology suffers in a special manner. I am not referring to the mere subservience that this habit betokens. That would be a most superficial reason for concern.[3] The real problem consists in the fact that our self-consciously European orientation has inhibited us from entering deeply into our own experience as a people. That is a serious charge, for it is tantamount to saying that it has inhibited us from becoming a genuinely theological community. Theology can occur only at the point where the tradition meets the spirit that informs a culture. I understand a theologian to be one who has permitted his own soul to become the place where that tradition and that spirit struggle with one another. The communication of the struggle as it is experienced elsewhere and by other people is not theology, however valuable it may be for the life of the ecumenical church.

Perhaps there is no more pathetic illustration of the tendency of theology on this continent to borrow the struggle, already articulated, from Europe than is provided in connection with the so-called neo-orthodox movement, more particularly its center, Karl Barth. I refer to this, not only because it provides a rather notorious example of the dangers of this practice, but also for its relation to what will follow.

The experience of existence which gave rise to the "theology of crisis," as it was first called, was not *our* experience. For sensitive Europeans, as so many of them have testified, the nineteenth century came to an end on August 1, 1914. A few—certainly Barth—had already sensed the demise of modernity even before the guns of August announced it openly. For us in North America, however, the

---

[3] I am not interested in the brand of indigenous and nationalistic concern which wants to be "American" (or "Canadian!") for reasons fundamentally extrinsic to Christian faith and theology. It is probably in some ways good that we have listened to the Europeans in theology and other disciplines, for when we have taken on self-consciously nationalistic ambitions of that sort, we have shown ourselves capable of notorious mediocrity and poverty of imagination.

modern epoch is only now beginning to crumble—though it does so with an accelerating pace that is truly frightening. In the decades between Barth's *Römerbrief* and the sense of a crisis as it has finally come on us, too, it was the unlikely fate of Barth and other Europeans around whom the radical theology of crisis developed to father in North America a new conservativism, a new "orthodoxy." And even the few North American Christians who had begun very soon after the First World War to permeate the depths of our own cultural and spiritual poverty (one thinks primarily of Reinhold Niebuhr)[4] were made advocates of this same reactionary development. Lacking inward acquaintance with the crisis of humanity that engendered this theology of crisis, and impressed mainly by the fact that this theology dared to go behind modernity in its attempt to understand the crisis, the majority of North Americans could only conclude that it was indeed a backward-looking movement; and they lined up for or against it accordingly. Thus one had the spectacle, which can only be regarded with deepest irony, of a theology that arose in response to the cataclysmic end of the nineteenth century being supported in North American circles mostly by people who had not yet entered the nineteenth century, many of them having a special religious affinity with the sixteenth, and being repudiated on the other hand by those who still supposed that mankind was on the upward way.

This example of the manner in which the European orientation of theology on this continent has deterred us from indigenous theological reflection provides a clue, at the same time, about where we might look for an explanation of why we have been content to adapt European trends. It is not necessary to exclude the factor to which allusion has already been made: the doctrinal and ecclesiastical authority of the parent church. But the reason for our specifically theological adherence is, I think, more subtle and more basic: never before have we been in grave doubt about the identity the parental culture gave, and in many ways still gives, us. Never before have we

---

[4] Only—or chiefly—the name of Niebuhr has caused me seriously to question my thesis that we have had an indigenous theology. It is true that Tillich also understood much about our continent; and despite the differences between his own and Niebuhr's theology, both of them comprehended the predicament of modern man in the light of a theology of the cross. But Tillich is marked by his European origins. And Niebuhr's *theology*, as distinct from his social ethics, has, I feel, not yet been understood or influential enough to warrant its being regarded a challenge to the thesis in question. I would be happy to think that what I have said in this essay is in its entirety inspired by the theological and historical analysis of Reinhold Niebuhr.

questioned the destiny first envisaged for us by those who discovered "America," that is, those European intellectuals who saw in this continent the stage on which the new man they heralded would enact his enlightened role. We have accepted that destiny, and have embellished it with high religious significance. Until now, we have not been driven to ask whether the vision of modernity upon which we were founded could be a delusion; and so the sense of the tragic and of an ending, which has been a powerful force behind all dynamic theological reflection, has not been conspicuously present to us. We have been more or less cognizant of the failure of the modern vision within Europe itself; and our theological interest in Europe has stemmed in part, on the positive side, from the suspicion that out of that failure there emerged a certain depth of theological authenticity lacking in our situation. At the same time, we have been able until now to believe that the failure of modernity in Europe was due to accidental factors, such as national ambition, overcrowdedness, the backwardness of certain peoples, and in general that proximity to the past and the primitive which even enlightened European nations could not shake. Thus we have known how to ask critically about Europe; but heretofore we have not been driven to ask critically about the dream European intellectuals once dreamt and generations of immigrants made lively, the dream called America. Until now, we have not had the occasion radically and in significant numerical seriousness to question the basic tenets of the modern epoch, the flowering of which was supposed to occur here.

But now the occasion has arrived. It has been ushered in, dramatically enough, by Vietnam, by the crisis of human survival, and by the notorious failure of our institutions. And it is accompanied by the no longer polite demands of the world's hungry that this continent, in particular, should examine itself with a view to repentance. The times call for original thought from many quarters in North America, not only from theology. But theology on this continent could evade the call to enter into the depths of this new confrontation with ourselves as a people only at the expense of irrelevance and disobedience. There are many within the ecumenical church, especially in the Third World, who are waiting to hear how North American theology will acquit itself in relation to this demand for indigenous thought.

The occasion for indigenous theological reflection comes to us, however, not only in the imperative but also in the indicative mood, that is, as an unprecedented opportunity. If it were seized upon with courage and imagination, Christians on this continent today could offer a theological perspective more profound in its understanding of the human condition, and more pertinent as gospel for that condition, than anything we could learn from old Europe.

My rationale for such an enthusiastic statement of the opportunity given us in this time is not to be found in any excessive estimate of our abilities; it relates rather to the character of our experience, which is unique in the modern world. It is stated rather succinctly in the following excerpt, again from Grant's essay "In Defence of North America"; it is the penultimate conclusion of the essay:

> We live then in the most realized technological society which has yet been; one which is, moreover, the chief imperial center from which technique is spread around the world. It might seem then that because we are destined so to be, we might also be the people best able to comprehend what it is to be so. Because we are first and most fully there, the need might seem to press upon us to know where we are in this new found land which is so obviously a "terra incognita."[5]

Only those who have entered deeply into the North American experience are in a position to explore what it means to have come to the end of human possibilities as these were envisaged by the architects of the modern epoch. Only they can ask with ultimate seriousness whether at the end of an era that optimistically proclaimed the ultimate mastery of man over nature it is still possible to speak of hope. For those who have not participated in the North American experience, or who participating in it have shrunk from following it to the precipice on which it stands today, the temptation to cling to the vision of human mastery continues to be strongly present. It is present today even among peoples who, like the Germans far more dramatically and conclusively than we, have been shorn of all the assumptions on which that image of man was based: the progressive view of history, the perfectibility of human society, the victory of rationality over evil, etc. In particular one aspect of the vision of human mastery continues to haunt even those whose experience of the world has been bitter: technology.

Only in North America has the experience of technological existence been full enough and long enough for people to know that technology does not solve all human problems and bring the good life. For Europeans, even many who have become disenchanted with other promises of the modern world, there remains an almost innocent fascination with technology, amounting very often to an implicit trust

---

5 *Op. cit.*, p. 40.

in technological salvation. Indeed, if "America" still represents to the European a certain redemptive possibility (and it does), it is largely because he is still able to regard this continent, despite its cultural naiveté, as a triumph of human technique. This is so not only for affluent nations like West Germany, which pattern themselves without shame on the American technocratic model; it also pertains for nations of Marxist persuasion, whose own acknowledged goals are spelled out clearly enough in the same language of technique which informs our own dominant culture, with variations only with respect to questions of distribution. After all its agony of spirit, after the physical and psychic suffering through which it has had to pass for more than half a century, Europe still clings to technology, the last offspring of the *imago hominis* that began with man's realization that he could measure nature. Technological salvation is what remains of the European dream called America.

But in North America itself it is possible to know, and to know very well, that also and precisely that last vestige of the dream is vastly deceptive. Not only has technology failed to produce the good life, but it has introduced factors which can only be regarded detrimentally and with fear and trembling. In Russia, where technological salvation runs very high, millions of men and women dream of owning automobiles, and think that happiness means the mobility and privacy cars could give them. We have possessed automobiles now, in most families, for three or four generations; and we know that automobiles bring human isolation, neurosis, and death with more regularity than they bring happiness. Beyond that, we face a future in which not only the automobile but other advanced technology has contributed to a scarcely habitable atmosphere and depletion of vital resources. At a deeper level of awareness, we have learned—as those not in possession of our technological experience have not learned—that the gravest problems we face in the contemporary world are such as to admit of "no technical solutions," as Garrett Hardin has phrased it.[6] And at a still deeper level, many of the more sensitive observers of our culture have understood for long that a people which looks to technique for salvation has ultimately to submit itself to the technological processes in which it puts its trust. For finally, as George Grant has put it, the mastery of nature has to mean the mastery of human nature.[7] Thus when B.F. Skinner says that we can no longer afford

[6] "The Tragedy of the Commons," reproduced in many places; e.g., Robert Leo Smith, ed., *Ecology* (New York: Harper & Row, 1973), pp. 382–90.
[7] *Op. cit.*

113

freedom and dignity for man he has merely announced what was implicit from the outset in the vision which inspired our civilization.[8]

To have participated in the experience of this continent—to have followed it into these present dark days—is to have discovered that there is no more America in the mythic sense of the term. There is no New World free from the sins of the fathers. Here, where the fathers of modernity said that a new humanity could emerge, and where time was granted, and resources, and peace for the unfolding of these possibilities, we have come upon the "original sin" in the very heritage of our founding fathers. Imagining ourselves masters in accordance with their blessing, we have come at last to the place where we shall have to lay down our freedom before the very processes of our mastery . . . or else find another birthright!

II. The Problem

The best works of man, said the survivor of Auschwitz Elie Wiesel, were born in the night. There is in our situation not only an occasion for indigenous theological thought, but the prospect of theological wisdom, wisdom of the sort that has not yet been granted us as a people or as a Christian community. But this prospect depends on something extremely problematic: the willingness and ability of enough numbers of people on this continent to enter into the night, consciously to take on themselves the task of exploring the meaning of the failure of this dream.

Just that, however, is what is most difficult for North Americans to do. Not only has our attachment to the modern vision robbed us of a frame of reference for the experience of the night; that attachment has also cut us off from alternative visions of existence on the basis of which we might have gained perspective for the comprehension of our condition. As George Grant has said, one could suppose that, since we are the most fully realized technological empire ever to have been, we should be best equipped to pursue the meaning of the technocratic existence. But, as he continues (and this is the concluding statement of his essay "in defense" of North America):

> Yet the very substance of our existing which has made us the leaders in technique, stands as a barrier to any thinking which might be able to comprehend technique from beyond its own dynamism.[9]

---

[8] Cf. B. F. Skinner, *Beyond Freedom and Dignity* (New York: Knopf, 1971).
[9] *Op. cit.*, p. 40.

To comprehend our condition, it is necessary to have access to a position outside our condition—something which has been understood, in groping and sometimes pathetic ways, by many of our young. But even to make the decision to go beyond the rubrics of modernity for the sake of comprehending it is far beyond the capacities of the majority; it can only be witnessed by them as a betrayal. The dominant culture of our society is committed to the *imago hominis* of the modern epoch at psychic depths which are truly abysmal. So exclusive is their attachment to the religion of mastery that most people in our society, even if they achieve some measure of self-knowledge and begin to suspect that the problems are directly related to our "doing," can only offer other kinds of "doing" (usually technological) as alternatives. We have been conditioned to believe that the modern epoch—and therefore that we—are the pinnacle of the process towards which time has been moving. It is psychically almost inconceivable for us, even when the possibility exists intellectually, to behave as if another culture, earlier or less "developed" than ours, could shed any light whatever on the meaning of our experience.

And still more complicating is the fact that the world-view by which we have been driven from the outset has conditioned us to think positively about existence. No society ever before in history dared to think so positively as we. To entertain the negative (the Night!) by which we are actually engulfed today is a spiritual feat of which most North Americans are simply not capable. We have no frame of reference, no *mythos*, for such an experience of negation. It is well known that we are incapable of coping even with the inevitable negative of life which comes to each of us as individuals; we have developed an elaborate and repressive institution and language world unique in history for dealing with death. How could we be expected to behave differently with respect to an omega factor which raises the spectacle of macrocosmic death? We have done our best to reduce that omega to manageable proportions, so that by now it is not uncomfortable to speak of "pollution," "the population problem," and even "famine" at polite dinner parties. What we face is nevertheless not any one of these things but a dreadful interacting of them all amounting to nothing less than a crisis of survival. And we have not become wholly serious about our situation until we have drawn the conclusion that precisely our "way of life" has contributed vastly to the crisis.

While our psychic commitment to the positive outlook urges us from within to repress the experience of negation, our institutions—

the incarnation of the fantasies of those who dreamt of man's mastery—offer us every assistance in doing so. The exhortation to think positively, to eliminate the negative, and not to mess with the ambiguities of history is put to us ever more insistently and in ever more vulgar form. It is not accidental in such a society that the so-called Disney World with its papier-maché spears and its forced positivism can attract greater and greater numbers of people. The 'Disney World' is infinitely preferable to God's, where the spears are real, and where presidents do not rise from their chairs, like Disney's President Lincoln, and put everything to rights again.

The owl of Minerva takes its flight only at evening, said Hegel. We stand on the threshold of wisdom. After a long history of borrowed struggles and assumptions, we could come to know ourselves; and that could be a saving knowledge for ourselves and many others. But the very thing that could bring us as a people to wisdom, namely the readiness to acknowledge and enter into the depths of our own night, is prevented by our neurotic attachment to a world-view in which there is and must be no night.

Christians hearing this analysis (and not a few have managed to hear it) are sometimes prone to jump to the conclusion that the situation signals a new "relevance" for Christianity. For has not Christianity dealt exactly in this encounter with the problematic? Is it not just the genius of Christianity to speak to those who sit in darkness and in the shadow of death?

One wishes that it were possible to proceed straightway to such an affirmation and to its elaboration. But to do so—as many seem willing enough to do—is to ignore a whole dimension of the problem: for Christians, indeed, the most frustrating aspect. For what must be said on the contrary is that just Christianity, as it has manifested itself in the life of this people, gives evidence of the same *fundamental* incapacity for the negative that informs the culture at large. It may indeed be that Christianity, more than any other influence, has contributed to our cultural propensity for eliminating the negative. Perhaps the basic genius of Christianity in North America, the thing which has kept it alive (relatively speaking) long after industrial Europe lost interest, has been its skilful adaptation to the positive outlook of modernity.

But we must be subtle. It would be wrong to interpret this as if it meant that the typical Christianity of North America has merely *disregarded* the negative. Indeed, from one point of view it could accurately be said that the negative has been its pre-occupation. For it

116

has occupied itself with nothing so much as with the transformation of the negative. Whether liberal or conservative, individualistic or communally oriented, the gospel by which the churches have lived on this continent is one which performs the same rudimentary service for man: namely, rendering positive life's negatives.

It would be short-sighted to associate this practice with its more outlandish forms only, such as the cult of positive thinking emanating from the Marble Collegiate Church in New York. What Norman Vincent Peale offered to the public was not an aberration, but the distillation of a more complicated but essentially identical gospel which has informed our entire continental experience. The representative man Richard Nixon understood this perfectly well when he named as his two favorite theologians Peale and Billy Graham. Both are eloquent, although quite different, spokesmen of the same religious positivism. They choose different forms of the negative on which to fasten, and different languages and exercises for exorcising it. But the fundamental thrust of their messages is the same, namely, the alleviation and removal of the experience of negation. That is what salvation means. And while it is certainly possible to find more sophisticated interpretations of it, it is extremely difficult to discover in our corporate experience instances of Christian proclamation which do not assume that just this transforming and eliminating of the negative is the function and task of Christianity.

What is inimical to this Christianity is not the negative as such, but the sustained experience of negation. It is unable to entertain an *unresolved* negative.

It could be said with a high degree of probability that the so-called great preachers of our history have all made their reputations on the basis of sensitive and articulate comprehension of the negating factors in the lives of men and women. But it would be precisely necessary in the first place to specify, in just that way, that their concentration was upon the *personal* experience of negation; comparatively few in our tradition have addressed themselves to the negating powers within our corporate, cultural, economic, and political existence. And in the second place it would be necessary to notice that the reputation of such men was not founded on their sympathetic comprehension of the negative alone. There is no better illustration of the insistence, within the churches, that every statement of the negative must be *resolved* than the outcry that is lifted today against the few in our churches who have really occupied themselves with exploring the negative before they dare to answer it with a triumphant positive.

117

There is however in this practice an implicit flaw, which, given certain circumstances, must begin to be conspicuous. These circumstances have in fact come on us as churches today; and in prospect of discovering that flaw there lies the possibility that we may discover, at long last, a different theology.

What I mean is this. It can be observed about everyone who sets about to provide answers that he regularly defines problems by the capacity of his answers to satisfy them. This is indeed the whole basis of the technological salvation about which we have already reflected. A problem is defined as such by reference to the technical solution required to speak to it. Problems defying technical solution are regularly ruled out as nonproblems: they cannot summon the necessary degree of empirical data to give them the status of a problem.

There is a certain willingness in human society to accept this fiction, and, as I have already suggested, this willingness amounts to a psychic necessity at times when life becomes extremely problematic. People need to hear that their problems are understood and to believe that they are soluble; therefore, they lend a special credence to those who can offer credible versions of this method.

There comes a point, however, where this process becomes overwhelmed by reality. Problems refuse to be silenced by answers. The conquering positive is impressive only in theory; life itself throws up too many negatives. Men cease to lend their credence to the system, for it has become all too obvious that it does not do what it claims to do. The Emperor has no clothes . . . or, perhaps, the clothes have no Emperor!

Christianity on this continent has never been known for its willingness to take on overwhelming human problems. It has usually shied away at the theological level, for example, from the problems of evil and suffering, except for rather domestic versions of the same. This has been partly due to the fact that it did not have the grand historical and natural displays of evil and suffering which have been visited on other peoples (except for the blacks; but then they had another theology, too!). But it has also been at the theoretical level, because of the commitment of North American Christianity to a version of historical existence which denied in principle the possibility of the tragic, and found that concept supported especially in the Christian declaration of the resurrection. Because it has been an answering theology, the Christianity of this continent has enjoyed a certain longevity, beyond that of the mother churches of Europe, which were more interested in announcing than in answering. But the very habit of answering has become the downfall of the churches in North America. For what has been happening increasingly in our midst is that the negative experiences to which we are being subjected are so numerous, various, and complexly interwoven that they overwhelm every attempt at resolution. More and more people, even among the Middle American segment for whom the churches have been sanctuaries against the night, find Christian answering unconvincing and simplistic. There is a recurrent and irrepressible sense that the problem has not been taken seriously enough.

The search for an alternative theology can begin at the point where this sense is permitted to grow; where one faces that the problematic of contemporary man cannot be resolved within the terms of reference of positive religion.

Many who have reached that point already in our midst have found no alternative posture *within* the Christian faith. Some have given up faith of every kind, finding that they could only curse God and die—or, in the modern translation of Camus, "think clearly and hope no more." Others, perhaps a greater number, have turned to the realm of pure spirit: they seek the answers to historical existence beyond history. In reality that is not an alternative, but a well-known variation on the theme: it merely transfers the negating of the negation to another world, thus providing a rationale for the abandonment of this one.

The question for one who refuses to adopt the solution of a flight from history, on the one hand, and on the other cannot curse God and die, can only be: is there a gospel which, without offering unbelievable earthly answers or unacceptable heavenly ones, will nevertheless help me to live in this world without ultimate despair? Is it possible to discover a faith that does not require me to repress the unbelief that rises up in me as I contemplate the present and future of the world? Is it possible to hope without embracing the official optimism of this society and of its religion?

The task of theology in North America today as I conceive it is to foster a climate within and beyond the churches where this question is possible.

III. The Possibility

In another of his books, George Grant has written that to question the technocratic assumptions of our culture is to enter a strange new world.

> So pervasive and deep-rooted is the faith that all human problems will be solved by unlimited technological development that it is a terrible moment for the individual when he crosses the rubicon and puts that faith into question. . . . One can thereafter only approach modern society with fear and perhaps trembling and, above all, with caution.[10]

To this I would add that for the Christian who questions the technocratic and positivistic assumptions of modernity as these are reflected in official Christianity, it is no less a matter of crossing the Rubicon with respect to the ecclesiastical and theological conventions of that Christianity. However, what this questioning may also do is to open the Christian to a possibility that is almost brand new for us, namely, the possibility of an original encounter with the roots of the Christian tradition, free from the molds into which modernity had thrust it. The questioning of modernity, including the Christianity that is inextricably bound up with it, *could* mean the possibility of hearing the gospel for the first time liberated from the triumphalistic assumptions of modern Western man. Once such a possibility has been seriously entertained, its implications become quite staggering. The recognition that the Christian faith has been used by modernity is no less revolutionary a discovery than Luther's or Marx's realization of the captivity of Western culture by economic capitalism. In the Third World today Christians are speaking of the fate of Christianity in the affluent nations of the West as "the ideological misuse of the Christian faith." It is particularly for Christians in North America to try to extricate the faith from the ideology, the wheat from the chaff. That would be the primary critical function of an indigenous theology.

Finally, we may outline that function with respect to three aspects of theological work: the theological, the ethical, and the ecclesiastical.

(1) The primary theological task of an indigenous theology in North America is to provide a frame of reference for the prolonged and intense experience of negation.

We have concentrated on being an answering theology, and this is our undoing in an age when answers can only have a hollow ring. Now we must concentrate on providing a place to which to refer the questions. Not the overcoming of the negative, but the possibility of engaging it, of encountering it at the level of consciousness, of facing it in all of its enormity, should be our endeavor. Our culture is sick, and because it is also very powerful its sickness infects the whole

---

[10] George Grant, *Philosophy in the Mass Age* (Toronto: The Copp Clark Publishing Company, 1966), pp. vii–viii.

world. On the brink of overt nihilism in our public life, and neuroti-
cally clinging to the positive in our private existences, we fear above
all an open confrontation with the contradiction between our highly
optimistic expectations and our increasingly depressing experiences.
The repression of this contradiction is costly in life and truth. Its
repression at home inevitably means that it breaks out in strange
places with names which quickly become household words: Vietnam,
Bangladesh, Chile. There can therefore be no more responsible theology, both at the political and the pastoral level, than one which tries
to provide a climate in which men and women in this society may feel
able to expose themselves to that contradictory state. Is it possible to
discover in the tradition of Jerusalem a way through which we may
enter into our own night? Or is Christianity so irrevocably positive
that its forays into the twilight zone must always be accompanied by
plentiful supplies of ersatz light?

The pursuit of such a question would take us inevitably to the very
center of the Christian proclamation. For in the last analysis, the
Christian positivism of our continent, whether in its liberal this-
worldly or its conservative other-worldly version, has been determined
by the theological decision that the message of and about Jesus is to
be received as a statement of triumph over that which negates. And
who could question such a decision? It seems altogether axiomatic.
But what *can* and *must* be disputed is the extent to which the biblical
declaration of the triumph of God in Christ has been colored and
distorted by its association with the triumphalistic pretensions of
white Western man. To what has the whole language of theology been
conditioned by Western imperialistic culture? What precisely *is* meant
by the victory of the Christ?

There can be little doubt concerning the meaning assigned to the
resurrection by the positive religion of our society: it has been the
primary theological foundation of the cultural assumption that the
negative, the *nihil*, the night, radical evil is basically unreal, nonexistent, a mere phantom. The fact that the theology of resurrection
on this continent has never been able to free itself from entanglement
with the Hellenistic concept of immortality of the soul is one piece of
evidence for this. At the sociological level, so is the fact that Easter
Sunday still draws many worldlings who otherwise do not darken the
churches' doors. And then the manner in which Easter has been
inextricably bound up with the conformity of nature—with lilies.
Everything has been done, so to speak, to ensure that this Easter
triumph lies not only within the realm of *possibility* but within the

realm of *necessity*. It becomes a matter not of unheard-of grace, but of *nature*. But precisely that has been its nemesis at last, because it now appears rather openly that there is nothing necessarily triumphant either in the realm of nature.

The critical theological task of an indigenous theology would be to extricate the biblical confession of the divine triumph for man from the triumphalistic anthropology of Western bourgeois culture. It is difficult to say how this could be achieved. After sixteen generations of the marriage of the divine glory to the kingdoms of this world and the glory of them, one has seriously to wonder whether the remnant of Christendom is capable, at the emotional level, of such a divorce. The disease of triumphalism is chronic with us. In North America it is doubly so, for with us the *de facto* cultural establishment of the Christian religion has been far more effective than the *de jure* administrative establishments of old Europe.

One thing seems certain: if it could be achieved, it would have to entail a radical reinterpretation of basic categories of theology. Faith, for example. Whatever the real triumph may mean concretely—the *gloria Dei* rightly divided from Western man's delusions of grandeur—it can only be an object of faith, namely the faith that is "not sight." For our own and future generations, that the glory of God is the object of faith and not sight must connote that we have to live with the prospect of an omega which bears none of the earmarks of an *implicit* alpha: a cross without a *necessary* resurrection, whether logically or existentially necessary. We can only open ourselves realistically and honestly to the experience of negation if we rid ourselves of doctrinal assumption which insulates us *a priori* from genuine exposure to the negative. The alternative to a necessary resurrection, however, is not, as we are conditioned to think, the acceptance of death and the impossibility of salvation, but a reinterpretation of resurrection faith in terms of possibility. The alternative to certainty, the certainty of a theology of glory which guarantees in advance a happy issue out of all our sufferings, is not, as we are conditioned to think, despair, but hope. We in North America shall be able to discern this hope—the hope that is against hope (Rom. 4:18)—if we allow ourselves to be carried into the wilderness where hope as we have understood it seems dead.

To say that the primary theological task of an indigenous theology is to provide a frame of reference for the experience of negation is not in essence different, then, from saying that our task is to devise a theology of hope. But not a hope which is borrowed from the quite different struggles of another people (whether in Europe, or in South America), and not a hope which merely ends by confirming the much-beleaguered national philosophy of optimism—and so had better not be called hope. The only hope that would be pertinent to our condition and responsible within the context of the contemporary world would be one born out of an encounter with the despair implicit in and emanating from our own way of life. That is no hope, in the Christian sense, which only shields persons from the meeting with death and despair.

(2) The primary ethical task of an indigenous theology in North America would be the development of theological foundations for raising and meeting the question of limits.

To cite George Grant once more:

> Surely the twentieth century has presented us with one question above all: are there any limits to history making? The question must be in any intelligent mind whether man's domination of nature can lead to the end of human life on the planet, if not in a cataclysm of bombs, perhaps by the slow perversion of the processes of life.[11]

Christian morality on this continent has had a good deal to say about the limits which pertain in personal life. But at the level of public morality it has been as expansionistic as the culture at large, and perhaps the primary cultic source of the culture's expansionism. Even the social gospel, which did break out beyond the confines of personal morality, did not ask about the limits of our mastery. On the contrary, it was impelled by the concern that we deploy our mastery more bravely and towards more noble ends.

This could perhaps have been urged with right in the nineteenth century. But when it is put forward by Christians today as our special contribution to the problematic of the technological society it betrays an astonishing naiveté about the human condition today. Not only does it innocently imagine that technique is purely neutral, available at will for good or evil purposes, but it has failed to recognize the rudimentary lesson that history and nature have been trying to teach us about limits. There *are* limits to growth, and because we are not observing them as a people, there are other peoples of earth who suffer. They suffer in obvious ways (famine, for instance), and they suffer in subtle ways (chiefly by thinking it their right and destiny to imitate us). They will not suffer forever with quiet resignation. Nor

[11]   *Ibid.*

will nature do so. Both history and nature have already rebelled against our mastery, and we have seen only the beginning of their rebellion.

Our situation is this. We are put into the position of people who either must limit themselves or be limited. And the limits that we face are such that they call in question our entire historic experiment, which was based on the idea, not only of our own mastery, but of the limitlessness and infinite resiliency of that which we were called to master.

Consciously to pursue an ethic of limits, then, is to swim against the stream of our history as a people, and of our own Christian contribution to that history, and (what is still more complicating) of the present constituency of our churches. For we would be deceiving ourselves if we did not recognize that the economy of limitlessness and of "development" is strongly represented amongst the Christian congregations of North America. And why not? Have not the churches kept before men's eyes the vision of a society like the great banquet of the kingdom of God? Have we not urged them to press beyond the limits, to dare to seek the fulfilment of all wants? And have we seriously questioned the system which assumes that that fulfilling is best achieved by personal ambition? Or have we helped to make larger for them the world that is full of creatures crying for fulfilment—and not just bales of used clothing?

Whatever our Christian past has been, theology today is called to lay the foundations of an ethic of limits. To separate the wheat of the gospel from the chaff of its ideological captivity would mean to ask, as those who have never before asked it earnestly, what are the limits of human mastery? Precisely what is the relation between man and nature, according to biblical testimony freed from cultural assumptions? And in the same vein, precisely what is his responsibility and capacity for planning the future? Must everything be stated in the language of "doing," or will we only be truly serious about our humanity when, as Karl Jaspers[12] suggests, we have discovered the limits of our "doing?" What does the word "dominion" in fact connote—when it is reflected on—as one might have anticipated it should be—in connection with the biblical witness to the one we call *Dominus,* Lord? Above all, what does the authentic tradition of our faith mean when it calls man a *creature?* A nihilistic society, said Nietzsche, is one in which there are no limits; there is nothing that I may not do. Is

[12] Karl Jaspers, *The Future of Mankind* (Chicago: Univ. of Chicago Press Phoenix Books, 1961), p. viii.

it possible that the whole concept of creaturehood in the Hebraic-Christian tradition refers to possibilities that are accessible only where limits have been comprehended, and that when there is nothing that I may not do I have reached the ultimate in the *distortion* of my creaturehood?

The discovery of our limits on this continent is the *sine qua non* for world peace. For only through that discovery can we enter into solidarity with those who cannot pretend that there are no limits, and who have never been able to indulge in that fantasy. The fellowship on which the world depends for its peace—that is to say, for its survival—is a fellowship of beggars. Mastery is no fit image of man for a world like ours, where no one people can survive unilaterally. Until Christians have been able to communicate such a message and life-style to the people of this continent, they will be pursuing the same deadly path as the other institutions of this society. The ethic of limits has to be translated, not only into terms of personal and social morality, but into hard political terms. And there are no existing major ideologies, either of the right or the left, that can be depended on as vehicles of that ethic. It calls for the most original and lonely theological work the church in North America has ever been asked to do.

(3) Accordingly, the primary ecclesiastical task of the indigenous theology would be to equip a Christian community which is prepared to suffer.

To suffer! It could only come to that, in any case, if the theological and ethical aspects of the task had been taken up with any kind of seriousness. For at every point what is involved in the indigenous theology is a critical disentanglement of the faith from the thickly woven fabric by which it has been bound to the dominant culture of this continent. And that could not be done without pain, often intense personal suffering.

What is called for is nothing less than the disestablishment of Christianity. But it is no ordinary disestablishment; it has very little in common with the debates of yore which produced the longest word in the English language—antidisestablishmentarianism! For nowhere else in the world has Christianity ever achieved the degree and kind of establishment that has pertained in our continental experienced. The very fact that we avoided what was called establishment, that is, the structural, administrative, and economic protection of a specific ecclesiastical body, has concealed from us the meaning of the *de facto* establishment of the Christian religion on this continent—though others, like Jews, have not been so unaware of it. Ours has been an establishment far more real than occurred in medieval Europe, as is evidenced by the fact that many more North Americans are prepared today to identify our way of life and Christianity than could be found in Europe. Ours has been a subtle, almost imperceptible establishment, because it is not at the level of form but at the level of content: namely, the faith itself has been identified with the highest aspirations of this culture.

And it has been the faith that has suffered in this marriage. For what was systematically removed from it, because it was so highly incompatible with our cultural assumptions, was just that element I have been calling here the negative. The dialectical tension that runs throughout biblical faith—a tension between good and evil, judgment and love, faith and unfaith, life and death; a tension whose resolution is indeed the promise of salvation, but of a salvation that is itself comprehensible only within the eschatological, dialectical tension of experience and expectancy—this biblical tension has been altogether dismissed by the typical Christianity of our culture, in favor of the positive element within it: that is, in favor of the element within it which modernity could consider positive.

And here we are able to glimpse something of the really pathetic plight of official Christianity in our time. The pathos of this Christianity is that in order to make itself amenable to modernity, it forfeited its only real asset for comprehending the contemporary. Having dispensed with what the tradition knew of as negative, unresolved, and full of pain, in order to embrace an undialectically triumphant positive, this Christianity gave away its only intrinsic capacity for comprehending and helping a people caught in a net of negativity amounting to covert nihilism, and unable to face it.

It is the critical task of an indigenous North American theology—so I have already claimed—to rediscover what the tradition knew about the abiding and recurrent negative. But that theological claim would not have been rightly grasped unless it were understood to connote, at the level of Christian existence, the equipping of a people for naked encounter with that negative. A people prepared to enter the wilderness and to be led to the edge of some Red Sea without knowing in advance that a way would open up. A people ready to go into the darkness of our epoch, without their pockets full of matches, candles, and fluorescent floodlamps. A people prepared to let the darkness penetrate also their own souls, and to be afraid. A people prepared to name the darkness—*our* darkness—even when it masquerades as heavenly light, and especially then. A people determined to look for light *within* the darkness, and not to cry for illumination and relief at the first signs of sunset. A people therefore prepared to call in question also what is—and undoubtedly will continue to be—the compulsive need of the religious to offer Jesus Christ as a refuge from the night. And so . . . a people prepared to suffer.

IV. Conclusion

No theology begins *de novo*. Nor does anyone discover an authentic theology just by entering into the darkness of his own epoch. We cannot dispense with the testimony of the past—its testimony to the darkness and to the light that shines in the darkness. But the testimony of the past is not just the testimony of our own past, fortunately. It is not just the testimony of triumphalistic Christianity.

There is a thin tradition, which however insignificant has never quite been overcome by the broad tradition which has informed Constantinian Christianity in its several guises. Luther[13] named it *theologia crucis*, the theology of the cross. What I have said about the possibility of an indigenous theology, I have wanted to say within that thin tradition. I have discovered in it a certain courage to go into the night of my generation, a night which I think will become darker for the generation of my children.

There can be no thought of merely imitating or repeating that tradition as it was appropriated by one or more of its greatest exponents. It can only be a matter of guidance. To get this guidance, however, we have to go outside our own continental experience; because, apart from the blacks, this thin tradition has never made its influence felt in our Christianity. And I am tempted to think that there may be some connection between that observation and the fact

[13] Whether Luther himself was consistent in his determination to avoid a "theology of glory" is a point of debate. But at the outset of his career as a reformer he described the "theology of the cross" in these terms:

> (19) That person does not deserve to be called a theologian who looks upon the invisible things of God as though they were clearly perceptible in those things which have actually happened (Rom. 1:20).
> (20) He deserves to be called a theologian, however, who comprehends the visible and manifest things of God seen through suffering and the cross.
> (21) A theology of glory calls evil good and good evil. A theology of the cross calls the thing what it actually is. Heidelberg Disputation, reproduced in *Luther's Works* (Philadelphia: Muhlenberg Press, 1957), XXXI, 40–41.

that our theology on this continent has been so much a matter of imitation and translation. Sometimes, it is true, those who listened with special interest to Luther, and later to Kierkegaard and the early Barth,[14] divined something of the thin tradition called *theologia crucis*. But too often what they divined did not lead them into "our darkness," but rather prevented them from engaging in theology indigenously by providing them with a general, doctrinal, and so to speak "eternal" point of view above the specifics of historical existence. We do not need more Luther, or more Kierkegaard, or more Barth; and we do not have to wait for Moltmann's[15] current "theology of the cross" to take shape before we can engage in our critical theological task. There can be no doubt, I think, that what we are required to do now is to think and to live a theology of the cross. But it must be an *indigenous* theology of the cross.

[14] To have qualified the name of Barth in this connection with the adjective "early" is to have begged an important question of interpretation in contemporary theology. I have discussed this at some length in the W.S.C.F. publication, *Hope Against Hope* (Geneva: WSCF Books, ed. David L. Swain, Vol. 1, No. 3, 1971, Serial Number 3).

[15] Cf. Jürgen Moltmann, *The Crucified God* (New York: Harper & Row, 1974).

11. A Definitive Study Paper: A Christian Declaration on Human Rights

JÜRGEN MOLTMANN

I. Human Rights and the Tasks of the Church and Theology

In many places and cultures throughout the world, the rise of insights into the basic rights and duties of human beings has coincided with the understanding of the humanity of persons. What is involved here is not an exclusively European or Christian idea, although at the time of the Enlightenment, human rights, not independent of Christian influence, entered into the processes of constitution-making in Europe and North America, and so attained a worldwide political significance. Today, however, it is particularly the peoples of the Third World who, through their struggle for freedom and self-determination, have impressed upon all human beings and states the urgent necessity of recognizing and realizing fundamental human rights.

The declarations of human rights considered valid today in the United Nations (even though they have not been ratified by all member states) are to be found in the Universal Declaration of Human Rights of 1948 and in the International Covenants on Human Rights (The International Covenant on Economic, Social and Cultural Rights; The International Covenant on Civil and Political Rights; The Optional Protocol to the International Covenant on Civil and Political Rights) of 1966. We have to be aware, however, that on the basis of their various political, economic, and social histories, the nations emphasize and seek to realize different aspects of human rights. For example, under the influence of the misery caused by fascist dictatorships, the North Atlantic states have formulated *individual* human rights over against the state and society. In their struggle against capitalism and class rule, the socialist states have given pre-eminence to *social* human rights. The nations of the "Third World" are demanding the right to *economic, social, and political self-determination*. Human rights therefore cannot be viewed as abstract ideals, but must be looked at against the background of the suffering and of the present struggles of individuals, nations, and states.

The task of Christian theology is not that of trying to present once more what thousands of experts, lawyers, legislators, and diplomats in the United Nations have already accomplished. But neither can Christian theology allow itself to dispense with the discussion of and the struggle for the realization of human rights. On the ground of the creation of man and woman in the image of God, on the ground of the incarnation of God for the reconciliation of the world, and on the ground of the coming of the kingdom of God as the consummation of history, the concern entrusted to Christian theology is one for the humanity of persons as well as for their ongoing rights and duties. The specific task of Christian theology in these matters is grounding fundamental human rights on God's right to—i.e., his claim on— human beings, their human dignity, their fellowship, their rule over the earth, and their future. It is the duty of the Christian faith beyond human rights and duties to stand for the dignity of human beings in their life with God and for God.

The church, Christian congregations, and ecumenical organizations have the clear task and duty of identifying, promoting, and realizing human rights. Since they are neither private associations nor statutory authorities, yet must exist and work in the public eye, those Christian organizations can be expected to be less influenced by their self-interests, and to be better able to enter the struggle for human rights with less prejudice than other institutions. This is why one can expect from them self-criticism as well as criticism of the egoism of the nations, states, classes, and races in which they find themselves; hence one can also expect their witness to a human solidarity with all those who bear the human countenance and more particularly their willingness to stand up for those robbed of their fundamental rights and freedoms.

II. God's Claim on Human Beings

Christian theology, on the strength of biblical witnesses, is related to God's dealing with people in history. What is at issue here is the liberation and redemption of human beings from their sinful godlessness and their deadly inhumanity, and thus also the realization of their original destiny through having been created in the image of God.

According to the Old Testament, Christian theology reflects the liberation of Israel from slavery in Egypt, the covenant of the liberating God with the liberated community, and the rights and duties of the people of God which are implied in the covenant of freedom. Liberation, covenant, and the claim of God are the basic content of the biblical witness of the Old Testament, and indeed they are found in this order. They have decisive directional power for Israel and Christianity in particular, and exemplary significance for all human beings and nations. The human rights to freedom, to community, to dominion, and to the future are inseparable constituents of God's claim on human beings and the whole creation; they make up the inalienable dignity of human beings living in a covenant relation with God.

According to the New Testament, Christian theology reflects the liberation of human beings from sin, law, and death through the coming, the sacrifice, and the resurrection of Jesus Christ. In the lordship of the crucified Son of man, the vicious circle of evil, "which must bear ever greater evil," is broken through, and the freedom of the children of God begins to appear. *Liberation* through the vicarious death of Christ, the new *covenant* in his blood, and the new *rights and duties* of the fellowship which is composed of "slaves and freemen, Jews and gentiles, men and women" (Gal. 3:28) are the basic content of the biblical witness of the New Testament. Because in his coming, his sacrifice, and his resurrection, Christ is "the visible image of the invisible God," human beings in his fellowship become his brothers and sisters, and set out on the way towards the realization of their human destiny as the image of God in the world. Herein lie his grace and their dignity.

By reflecting the liberation, the covenant, and the claim of God according to biblical witnesses, Christian theology also discovers the freedom, the covenant, and the rights of human beings today, and therefore brings out the pain caused by their present inward and outward enslavements, as well as the struggle for their liberation from these enslavements, towards a life of dignity, rights, and duties in fellowship with God. In a world which is not yet the kingdom of God, Christians cannot leave any area of life without witness to the divine liberation, the covenant of God, and the dignity of human beings. The biblical witness to liberation, covenant, and God's claim leads to a corresponding Christian practice and theology.

The universal presupposition of the particular history of God's dealing with Israel and with Christianity is found in the reality that the God who liberates and redeems them is the Creator of all human beings and things. Thus in God's liberating and redeeming action the original destiny of human beings is both experienced and fulfilled. In the "image of God" concept, the divine claim on human beings is expressed. Human rights to life, freedom, community, and self-determination mirror God's claim on persons, because in all their relationships in life—human beings with each other and creatures with the creation—they are destined to reflect the image of God.

The universal purpose of Israel's and Christianity's particular experience of God is found in the reality that the God who liberates and redeems them is the fulfiller of the history of the world, who will bring his claim on his creation to realization in his kingdom. Thus his liberating and redeeming action in history reveals the true future of human beings; the "image of God" is their real future. In all their relationships in life—human beings with each other and creatures with the creation—they therefore have a "right" to future. Human rights mirror the claim of the coming God and of his future upon human beings.

God's claim on human beings was and is experienced in concrete events of the liberation of human beings, in their covenant with God, and in the rights and duties inherent in their freedom. Image of God, as destiny, points to God's indivisible claim on human beings and therefore to their inalienable dignity.

III. Fundamental Human Rights

By *fundamental* human rights we mean those rights and duties which belong essentially to what it means to be truly human, because without their being fully acknowledged and exercised, human beings cannot fulfil their original destiny of having been created in the image of God.

1. The image of God is human beings in all their relationships in life.

Human beings in the fulness of their life and in all life's relationships—economic, social, political, and personal—are destined to live "before the face of God," to respond to the Word of God, and responsibly to carry out their task in the world implied in their being created in the image of God. They are persons before God and as such capable of acting on God's behalf and responsible to him. As a consequence of this, a person's rights and duties as a human being are inalienable and indivisible.

Economy, society, and the state have to respect this dignity and responsibility of human beings, for their role as human beings, with rights and duties, comes before any constituting of society and

132

government. Respect for freedom of conscience is the foundation of a free society. Often in monarchical folklore and in political ideologies the king alone is called "the image of God." "The shadow of God is the prince and the shadow of the prince is the people" (Babylonian Mirror of the Princes). Only the ruler can function as mediator between the gods and the people. When the Bible calls human beings the "image of God," this constitutes a fundamental criticism of the divinization of the rulers and their ideologies of rule. Not the king, but the individual human being alone is the mediator between God and the people. Human beings do not exist for the sake of rule; rule rather exists for the sake of human beings.

From this follows the democratization in principle of every kind of rule by human beings over others. The rulers and the ruled must be recognizable in like manner, and in common as being human. This is possible only when there is an equality under the law for all citizens. A constitution (the covenant) must guarantee the fundamental human rights as basic rights of the citizens. It must bind together those who are ruling and those who are ruled. Only on the basis of equality under the law can expression be given to the common human identity of rulers and ruled alike. The human rights and duties implied in the image of God concept are honored in history through the constant, open, and incessant process of democratizing the shaping of the people's political will. The control of the exercise of rule through the separation of powers, the limitation of the mandate to rule to a stipulated period of time, and the extensive self-rule and participation of the people are the historically developed means for honoring the image of God present in human beings.

If human rights are based on God's claim on human beings and if human freedoms are rooted in liberation by God, then we also have to formulate the fundamental human duties without which those rights and freedoms cannot exist. Freedom and rights by themselves mean virtually nothing. Just as it is crucial to formulate the dignity and the rights of human persons over against the state in order to limit and control power, and to cooperate in its exercise, so it is equally important to heed the duties which correspond to these rights and which human beings must exercise for the sake of others. Among these duties we should mention in our present discussion the right to resistance and the duty to resistance against illegal, illegitimate, and inhuman regimes, in favor of the right of the neighbor.

According to the Reformed confessional writings, one is required to obey the authorities "insofar as they do not command that which

133

is contrary to God" (Zwingli, Zurich Disputation, 1523, Summatory Articles, No. 38). "Therefore all their laws shall be in harmony with the divine will . . ." (39). "But if they are unfaithful and transgress the laws of Christ they may be deposed in the name of God" (42). As a consequence of the divine covenant of freedom, human beings are called "to save the lives of innocents, to repress tyrannie, to defend the oppressed" (Scottish Confession, 1560, Article 14).

The rights which secure the freedom of the individual can only be observed if they are bound up with the corresponding duties of liberating those from whom these rights are withheld. Christian love honors the rights of the neighbor.

2. The image of God is human beings together with others.

Only in human fellowship with other people is the human person truly image of God (Gen. 1:28). The history of freedom in Europe and North America was one-sided in emphasizing the individual rights of the human person over against economic, social, and political organizations of rule. It is the error of liberalism to overlook the social side of freedom, and it is the failure of individualism to overlook the social consciousness that must correspond to the human personality. It is not against his or her fellow human beings, not apart from them, but only in human fellowship with them and for them, that the individual can correspond to his or her destiny as created in the image of God.

In fellowship before God and in covenant with others, the human being is capable of acting for God and being fully responsible to him. As a consequence of this, the social rights and duties of the human community are just as inalienable and indivisible as persons' individual rights and duties. Human beings have to heed the dignity and the responsibility of community in economy, society, and state, just as the latter has to heed those of the former. It does not follow from the "democratization" of the rule of human beings over others that every human being is his or her own absolute ruler. Just as according to Genesis 1:27 the image of God appears in the fellowship between husband and wife, so it is also represented in larger social contexts only through human fellowship. Thus the rights of human beings to life, freedom, and self-determination always arise together with the human community's claim upon people. In principle there is no priority of individual rights over social rights, just as conversely there is no priority of social rights over individual rights. Both stand in a genetic context of reciprocal conditioning, just as historically the

134

processes of the socialization and the individualization of people mutually condition each other.

The rights of persons can only be developed in a just society, and a just society can only be developed on the ground of the rights of the person. The freedom of the individual can only be constituted in a free society, and a free society can only be constituted on the ground of individual freedom. Human liberation is liberation for community, and human community is community in freedom.

Individual societies and states, in their social rights and duties, are responsible not only to the people who live in them but also to humanity. Human rights thus also entail humanity's claim on individual societies and people. If particular political and social communities are bound through their constitutions to the human rights of their citizens, they must also be bound, on the other hand, to the rights of humanity. Collective egoism threatens human rights just as much as individual egoism. Thus individual communities and states are only then really legitimized by human rights, when they respect not only the human rights of their own citizens, but also to the same degree those of other nations and peoples. Human right is indivisible; it is no privilege. Therefore national foreign policy can only be legitimized as the world's domestic policy. International solidarity in overcoming the horror of starvation and the threat of world military crises has, therefore, because of the rights of humanity, a precedence over loyalty to one's own people, to one's own class, race, or nation. Individual communities and states have human duties in the face of the rights of the whole humanity to life, freedom, and community. Therefore human rights point to a universal community in which alone they can be realized.

3. Being created in the image of God is the basis of the right of human beings to rule over the earth and of their right to community with the nonhuman creation.

In Genesis 1:28ff. the creation of human beings as the image of God is followed by the blessing of God and the human calling to be fruitful and rule over the nonhuman creation. Human rule over the earth is to correspond to the will and command of the Creator who loves his creation. Human beings are to "till and keep" the earth (Gen. 2:15) and to rejoice in it. Only where human dominion over the earth corresponds to the Creator's lordship over the world, do human beings fulfil their creation in the image of God. Plundering, exploitation, and the destruction of nature contradict their right and dignity.

Therefore human dominion over the earth includes a sense of community with the earth. Human rule is only then made legitimate when it is exercised in cooperation and community with the environment, and leads to life-giving symbioses between human society and the natural environment. The right of human beings to rule over the nonhuman creation must therefore be balanced by their respecting the "rights" of the nonhuman creation.

If the right to the earth is given to human beings, it follows that each and every human being has the basic economic right to a just share in life, nourishment, work, shelter, and personal possessions. The concentration of the basic necessities of life and the means of production in the hands of a few should be seen as a distortion and perversion of the image of God in human beings. It is unworthy of human beings and contradicts God's claim on them. The widespread withholding of basic economic rights, the impoverishing of whole peoples and population groups, and worldwide starvation caused by political and economic imperialism in our divided and strife-torn world, are a desecration of the image of God in people and of God's claim upon each and every person. Without the realization of the fundamental economic rights of human beings to life, nourishment, work, and shelter, neither their individual nor their social rights can be realized.

If, along with the right of human beings to the earth, "rights" of the earth over against human beings are recognized, then basic ecological duties are also bound up with these basic economic rights. It is not possible to increase basic economic rights at will simply by responding to increased demands, because economic growth is determined by ecological limits. The human struggle for survival and world domination cannot be carried out at the expense of nature, since in that case "ecological death" would anyway prepare the way for the end of human life altogether. Economic human rights should therefore be brought into line with the basic cosmic conditions for the survival of humanity in its natural environment. These rights can no longer be realized through uncontrolled economic growth, but only through the growth of economic justice within the "limits of growth." Economic justice in the provision and distribution of food, natural resources, and the industrial means of production will have to be directed towards the survival and the common life of human beings and nations. This is the only way of attaining ecological stability in mutual survival as well as in a common life alongside the nonhuman creation. Today economic and ecological justice mutually condition each other and thus can only be realized together.

4. Being created in the image of God is the basis of the right of human beings to their future and their responsibility for those who come after them.

Human beings in all their relationships in life—with each other and in community with the nonhuman creation—have as the image of God a right to self-determination and responsibility for their future. Their true future lies in the fulfilment of their being destined to the glory of their fellowship with God, with other human beings, and with the whole creation. In human history, with the kingdom of glory not yet realized, human beings correspond to this dignity for which they were created through their openness for this future and through their responsibility to the present if they attain the freedom of re- their "citizenship in the kingdom of God," through which they gain their dignity, human beings have a right to their true future as well as corresponding duties in the shaping of life in the present.

People can only make use of their right to this future and their responsibility to the present if they attain the freedom of responsibility and the right to self-determination. Self-determination and responsibility to the present in the face of the future relate (1) to human beings in all their relationships in life; (2) to human beings in community with others; and (3) to human beings in community with the nonhuman creation. This is an important dimension in the basic individual, social, economic, and ecological human rights and duties. There are no human rights in the present without the right to self-determination and one's own responsibility in the face of the future, for people live personally, collectively, economically, and ecologically in time and history. Their eternal and their temporal future therefore also have a "claim" on them. The political recognition and pursuit of human rights ultimately gain their significance in this perspective of the future. Human beings become free and affirm their rights and duties as their true and eternal future gains power over them in hope, and conditions their present. Thus, in accord with this future, they will stand up for the right to a temporal future and the right to life of those who come after them. They will struggle not only for justice in the world of their own generation, but also for the support and preservation of justice in generations that will follow. There exists not only a personal and a collective egoism, but also an egoism of the generations. Thus people should not exploit their present at the expense of the future, just as there is no obligation to sacrifice their present to the future. Rather, they will work for a just balance between the chances of life and freedom in the present and in the future generations. In a time of over-population and of the "limits of growth," this temporal perspective of human rights assumes particular significance. Economic politics, population politics, health politics and, under certain circumstances, genetic politics, should be directed towards the human rights of the present and coming generations.

IV. The Justification and Renewal of Human Beings

Human rights are only effective insofar as people are truly human and act humanly. Their inhumanity becomes manifest in the violations and abuse of human rights. This is why, behind the practical question as to how human rights may be realized on earth, there is the more profound question as to where people can experience their true humanity and how they can overcome their actual inhumanity.

Ever since the Universal Declaration of Human Rights in 1948, political violations of human rights have been brought to the awareness of world public opinion. This has brought to light how serious and widespread are the everyday violations of the fundamental rights of human beings through power politics and unjust authority, through hate and fratricide. The growing use of torture under dictatorships is a terrifying indication of the fact that the Declaration of Human Rights, and its public acceptance, have not in themselves created a new humanity among the nations. Nevertheless, the Declaration of Human Rights sharpens people's conscience and renders any inhumanity illegitimate.

Moreover, since the discussion on the International Covenants of 1966, it has become clear that human rights are not only violated but also abused. They are abused whenever they are used ideologically to justify private interests over against the rights of other human beings. They are abused whenever they are divided up, and it is pretended that only part of them stand for human rights in their totality. It is then that we see the birth of individual egoism, national arrogance, humanity's imperialism over against nature, and the absolutism of the present generation over against future generations. The increasing ideological abuse of human rights is one further indication that declarations and ratifications alone do not create true humanity among human beings. Nevertheless, insight into the indivisible totality of human rights sharpens the consciences and sense of responsibility of people for each other.

Christian theology uses the word "sin" to describe people's inhumanity, as it is made manifest in continued violations and abuse of human rights. According to the testimony of the Bible, human beings have themselves failed to come up to their original destiny to live as God's likeness on earth, and they still fail to do so today. They wanted to "be like God" and thereby lost their true humanness (Gen. 3; Rom. 5). Enmity therefore characterizes humanity's relationship to nature (Gen. 3), and with Cain's murder of his brother begins the history of a humanity that does not want to be its brother's keeper (Gen. 4). And so people's sin perverts their relationships with God, their creator; with their fellow humans, their neighbors; and with nature, their home. God to them becomes a judge, fellow human beings become their enemies, and they become estranged from nature. Today, fear and aggression dominate a divided and hostile humanity which is on the way to totally destroying itself and the earth. Human rights can only be realized when and insofar as the justification of unjust human beings and the renewal of their humanness take place.

The Christian faith recognizes and proclaims that God through Jesus justifies unjust human beings and renews them to their true humanness. Through the incarnation of Christ, God restores to human beings who want to "be like God" their true humanity which they had abandoned. Through the death of Christ, God takes the judgment of people's sin on himself and reconciles them to himself (2 Cor. 5:19). Through the raising of Christ from the dead, God makes real his claim upon people in that he justifies them (Rom. 4:25). Through the outpouring of his Spirit on all flesh (Acts 2), God renews his likeness on earth, unites a divided humanity and liberates his creation from the shadow of evil. In the coming of his kingdom, God will ultimately glorify his right, justify human beings and transfigure creation.

God's claim on human beings in this world of sin and inhumanity is revealed to Christians through the gospel of Christ (Rom. 1:16–17). Because the divine right of grace is proclaimed to all people through this gospel, the God-given dignity of each and every person is proclaimed in conjunction with it. But where this human dignity is revealed, fundamental human rights are also made to come into force. Their realization is made possible and becomes therefore an undeniable commitment.

On the strength of the gospel, human rights in a hostile and inhuman world are first and foremost made real through the service of reconciliation (2 Cor. 5:18ff.). Faith separates the human person from inhuman sin. Love accepts the person and forgives the sin. Hope perceives the human future of the person and opens up new life. In this way—through faith, love, and hope—humanity, once betrayed and lost, is restored to the people. Through the service of reconciliation, human dignity and right are restored in this inhuman world. Wherever people's dignity is recognized and their right restored, there this service of reconciliation takes place. Reconciliation is nothing less than justifying justice; it is the power of the new creation in this twisted world.

For the sake of reconciliation one can therefore forgo one's own right. For the sake of the neighbor's right, one can suffer up to the point of giving one's life. Selflessness and sacrifice in the "service of reconciliation" of the world with God are always also selflessness and sacrifice in the service devoted to the true humanity of people. Christians have the divine calling to bring the right of reconciliation to bear on the worldwide struggle for privileges and power, in which they are witnesses to the future and agents of hope. For with the right to reconciliation there begins here and now a process in which the present unrecognizable world changes into a world that will be seen to be a human world loved by God. The experience of reconciliation turns enemies into friends. Working at reconciliation opens up the future of life to people who are threatened by death. Sacrifices in the service of reconciliation are the seeds of hope. Without reconciliation, the humanization of situations as they are is impossible. Without their humanization, reconciliation remains ineffective. Reconciliation and change belong together, and together they bring about humanness in this world.

It is the task of Christians in the existing world conflicts in which they live to proclaim the gospel of justification, to live the liberating faith, to exercise the ministry of reconciliation, and to give in their congregations a demonstration of a reconciled humanity in the fellowship of men and women, Jews and gentiles, slaves and freemen (Gal. 3:28). It is especially when Christians fulfil these specifically Christian tasks that they serve the realization of humanity of all people. By proclaiming God's justifying justice they proclaim the dignity of human beings. By practicing the right of grace they practice basic human rights. The Christian faith therefore does not excuse us from the struggle for the recognition and realization of human rights, but leads us into this very struggle. The community which calls Jesus Son of man suffers under the ongoing inhumanity and dehumanization of human beings and in its prayers turns this suffering into a painful awareness.

V. Priorities and Balance in the Struggle for Human Rights

Because human beings as individuals, in community, and in humanity are meant to reflect the image of God, all human rights are bound up with and related to one another. One can neither curtail them, separate them from each other, or differentiate between them. Furthermore, all human rights are bound up with specific human duties. Rights and duties cannot be separated from each other; privileges should not grow out of rights nor empty demands out of duties.

But in human history, people and nations, responding to the needs in which they find themselves, always set priorities. When the economic need stands in the foreground, they seek first to realize basic economic rights. Where political oppression is reigning, they seek first to realize political rights. Every progress in one area of life, however, causes the structure of life to get out of balance. The one-sided, uncontrolled, and uncoordinated economic growth in some nations has pushed the political, social, and personal balance of human beings in these societies to the edge of destruction. The hegemony of the developed industrial nations has kept other nations in conditions of underdevelopment and has made them dependent. The sudden development and securing of personal freedoms and rights can weaken collective rights and duties, just as conversely the one-sided extension of collective rights can lead to the weakening of personal rights. Thus partial progress in one area of life must be constantly accompanied by the redressing of the balance of human rights in other areas. Progress without balance is destructive just as balance without progress degenerates. The real history of the recognition and realization of human rights is accomplished in the constant conflict between progress and balance, a conflict which cannot be solved within time.

Whoever honors human beings as the image of God must acknowledge all human rights in the same degree and therefore view them in their indissoluble relationship to each other. Whoever heeds the inalienable dignity of human beings must, in the conflict between progress and balance, look to the unity of human rights, the human rights of people in all their relationships of life, and the rights of the whole human race. It follows that in the one-sided progress in the

141

development of human rights in one area, human rights in another area of life should never be fundamentally suspended. To bring this partial progress in harmony with human rights then becomes an irrevocable demand, because otherwise the balance of the whole structure of life cannot be won back, nor can human dignity be wholly honored.

In the conflict of human history, people always live with a disturbed balance in their human rights. Their human dignity appears in a somewhat distorted form; therefore it is necessary, in order to realize the totality of human rights, to develop strategies which eliminate the inequalities inevitably resulting from established priorities. In countries which purchase their sudden economic progress at the expense of political rights and individual freedom, one must press for the realization of political and individual human rights. In countries which secure the personal freedoms of their citizens at the expense of the social rights of the community, these collective rights and duties must be promoted. In societies which have established social rights at the expense of individual rights, individual human rights are to be promoted. In dependent and underdeveloped countries, the rights of independence and self-determination have priority. The acknowledgment of the inalienable dignity of human beings and the insight into the indivisible unity of their rights and duties can be regarded as regulative ideas and in various situations and societies can establish priorities and produce balance.

On the basis of their various histories, individuals, peoples, and nations have given particular emphasis to differing aspects of human rights. They must establish their priorities in different ways in order to escape from inhuman conditions, from want, violence, and dependence; and so their concerns for human rights vary. However, the concept of the indivisibility and thus the unity of human rights should act as a pointer to the future of a universal established community of all people and nations. The right to different concerns must be integrated into the higher right of the just balance of concerns because without such balance humanity will not survive its conflicts.

Accordingly, the following can be expected from Christianity, churches, congregations, and ecumenical organizations:

1. In the struggle for human rights and political priorities they will represent the unassailable *dignity of human beings* and thus also the indivisible *unity of their human rights and duties.* Both are con-

stituted through the claim of the one God on persons in all of their relationships of life.

2. In various situations of people and nations, they will press for the *restoration of those particular human rights* which through one-sided progress and established priorities have become neglected, weakened, or repressed.

3. They will overcome their own egoism in order to *overcome the egoism* of individual, social, and human rights over against nature, and the egoism of the present generation over against the coming generations, and in order to serve the humanity of each and every person in the interest of God their Creator and Redeemer.

4. Through public proclamation and education they will sharpen the duties of the individual which are inexorably bound up with the rights of human beings with regard to their God-given dignity, to other people, to nature, and to the future.

Christianity understands itself as witness to the three-in-one God who liberates human beings from inward and outward inhumanity, who allows them to live in his covenant, and leads them to the glory of his kingdom. Christians therefore stand up for the dignity of human beings out of which emerge their rights and duties. For the sake of God they will stand up with all means at their disposal, acting as well as suffering, for the dignity of human beings and their rights as the image of God. For their service to the humanity of persons they need the right to religious freedom, the right to form a community, and the right to public speech and action.

12. Guidelines and Implications

The task of *Christian theology* is not that of trying to present once more what thousands of experts, lawyers, legislators, and diplomats in the United Nations have already accomplished. But neither can Christian theology allow itself to dispense with the discussion of, and the struggle for, the realization of human rights. On the ground of the creation of man and woman in the image of God, on the ground of the incarnation of God for the reconciliation of the world, and on the ground of the coming of the kingdom of God as the consummation of history, the concern that is entrusted to Christian theology is one for the humanity of persons as well as for their ongoing rights and duties.

I. Theological Guidelines

1. We understand the basic theological contribution of the Christian faith, in these matters, to be the grounding of fundamental human rights in God's right to, that is, his claim on human beings.

This is to say that human rights are ultimately grounded not in human nature; nor are they conditioned by individual or collective human achievements in history. They reflect the covenant of God's faithfulness to his people and the glory of his love for the church and the world. No earthly authority can legitimately deny or suspend the right

Prepared at the Theological Consultation, London, February 18–21, 1976. The consultation, led by Jan M. Lochman, was attended by Daniel von Allmen (Switzerland), Michael Bame (Cameroon), G. L. Barnes (Australia), David Botha (South Africa), Rubens Cintra Damiao (Brazil), C. M. van Heemstra (Netherlands), James Irwin (New Zealand), Brian Johansen (South Africa), R. Stuart Louden (Scotland), G. Meuleman (Netherlands), Allen O. Miller (USA), Jürgen Moltmann (Federal Republic of Germany), L. R. L. Ntoane (South Africa), Sam Prempeh (Ghana), Jong Sungh Rhee (Korea), and Willy A. Roeroe (Indonesia). Leopoldo Niilus, director of the WCC Commission of the Churches on International Affairs, was an observer. The Geneva staff included Richmond Smith and Fred Kaan.

and dignity of being human. It is in the light of this covenant as fulfilled in the cross and resurrection of Jesus Christ and in the power of the Holy Spirit outpoured upon all flesh that Christians express solidarity with all those who bear a human countenance, and more particularly, a willingness to stand up for those whose fundamental rights and freedom are robbed.

2. Our biblical faith commits us to a view of human life in its wholeness expressed in three basic complementarities: male and female, the individual and society, human life and its ecological context.

In the identification of our humanity as created in the image of God, we affirm
—the equal dignity and interdependence of man and woman;
—the equal validity and interdependence of personal rights (freedom and dignity) and social rights (justice and community);
—and the equal dignity and interdependence of the present generation and future generations in the stewardship of nature.

As humanity stands in a covenant relationship to God, that relationship carries with it covenant responsibilities in our stewardship of creation.

Further, we acknowledge
—the equal validity and interdependence of "my rights" and "the rights of my neighbor"; and
—the equal significance and interdependence of human rights and human duties.

3. Our biblical faith also warns us about the destroying powers we face in the struggle for the realization of human rights.

It has been aptly said that the only universal thing about human rights today is their universal violation. In the light of our biblical faith we are driven to acknowledge the extremity to which the image of God has been corrupted and distorted in our world.

Human rights suffer not only from their denial and abuse but from their partisan and polarized fulfilment. Witness the demonic compulsion of one human being or ethnic group to achieve self-confirmation by the dehumanization of others. Witness the demonic compulsion of states to tyrannize their citizens and exercise imperial dominion over other states. Witness the demonic compulsion of the powerful to implement their economic aggrandizement at the expense of nature, the poor of the earth, and the future of humanity. As a result we must confess that the exercise of human rights participates fully in the ambiguity of human life and can be destructive as well as creative, demonic as well as holy. Being human is being threatened by sin, Satan, and death. These threats are no respecters of human beings, and human rights are no match for their power. In anguish, fear, frustration, and despair humans cry out for salvation!

4. We boldly confess the liberating power of Jesus Christ and affirm the church's ministry of reconciliation and grace.

Though caught up in the experience of its own guilt and frustration and virtually impotent in the face of the demonic powers which enslave our sinful world, the church is nevertheless commanded to bear witness to the liberating power of Christ's cross and resurrection. Called to live and think in this perspective, Christian theology can contribute to the theory and practice of human rights by ministering the distinctive wholeness of the gospel bequeathed to the church, the word of reconciliation and grace!

In the struggle for human rights, there is no way to avoid conflict between different groups, particularly between the rich and powerful and the poor and powerless. The message of reconciliation, which must always be faithful to God's act of reconciliation in which his justice and love issue inseparably in action, does not obviate these conflicts. As the word of the cross, reconciliation means neither appeasement nor neutrality. Yet, it is the basic promise of the gospel that, in spite of the bitterness of the struggle and the suffering it entails, the final goal is the reconciled community within the one family of God.

The theological affirmation of God's right to, that is, his claim on human beings, as the foundation of human rights, opens the perspective of God's free grace as the ultimate perspective, transcending all our achievements and failures. This is particularly important for our struggles in the area of human rights. It prevents us from despairing in situations of overwhelming and frustrating setbacks, as we confront them in our contemporary world. At the same time, it prevents our involvement in the struggle for human rights from becoming a self-righteous justification by works, rather than a thoroughgoing repentance and self-giving investment in justice and freedom as a response to our having been justified by God's grace alone.

This spirit of "costly reconciliation" and "costly grace" represents the contribution of the Christian church to today's worldwide struggle to sustain and foster human dignity and human rights.

II. Some Practical Implications

The preceding theological theses and the arguments set out in Dr. Jürgen Moltmann's paper suggest many practical implications. Some of these appear in the form of four final points in Dr. Moltmann's paper. Others are outlined in what follows.

It must be emphasized that the following principles must be seen in the closest connection with the theological bases from which they have been derived. Like the preceding theological arguments, they are only offered as guidelines which might be useful in indicating possible ways of implementing human rights in different social, cultural and political contexts.

1. Principles relating to the internal life of the churches

The theological basis suggests that the Christian community of all realms should be one in which the dignity and rights of all men and women are fully recognized and implemented.

a. It is therefore recommended that all member churches should study the foregoing theological guidelines and hence relate them to further programs of action. In particular, such a study could be related to local conditions to determine whether special attention needs to be given to

—the rights of the individual;
—the rights of society as a whole;
—the rights to religious freedom;
—the rights relating to the environment;
—the rights of the generations following.

Individual member churches might take it upon themselves to make appropriate representations to their governments with a view to appealing for action where this is desirable.

b. It is recommended that member churches draw in those members of the community who through special knowledge, experience, and resources, or simply through concern, are able to serve the cause of human rights.

c. In that violations of human rights and the destruction of human relationships go together, attention should be given to the processes of reconciliation, taking cognizance of the fact that confrontation and pain are invariably necessary in order to expose the disabilities and cruelties under which people are suffering. The processes of reconciliation begin with the full recognition of the human dignity of the other in Christ.

147

d. In this way the Christian communities should strive for a realization of that kind of "alternative society," characterized by the marks of the kingdom of God, in which people can individually and collectively achieve their full human potential. The church will thus be a sign to the world of true human existence under the reign of Jesus Christ.

e. By faithfully respecting the dignity and rights of their fellow Christians the churches will promote that interdependence among themselves which is integral to a faithful representation of the new creation in which the image of God is being restored (Col. 3:10–11). Only thus can the witness of the church in the world become more credible and effective.

2. Principles relating to the external life of the churches

In that the church is part of the larger human community and represents that which the Christian faith believes to be potentially true for all humanity, it has inescapable responsibilities towards that wider society.

a. In relation to society and culture:

There is a need to expose the root causes of the brutal and subtle violations of human rights which are increasing rather than decreasing. The general principle would be the tendency of one group to dominate another. This domination is often rationalized and even "justified" on ideological, religious, racial, and even sexual grounds, insofar as women suffer serious disabilities in comparison with men in most societies. The churches could engage in active programs of investigation into these possible problems, since those who are suffering are often the most inarticulate.

As freedom of conscience and religious practice are paramount in the understanding of humanity as created in the image of God, the Christian church should at all times appeal for this freedom for all. This is the necessary implication of that freedom which it desires for itself, not in order to indulge in self-centered privilege but in order to be of service to the society of which it is a part. By engaging in this service Christians in situations of relative freedom will express their solidarity with those experiencing oppression (cf. further the final paragraph of Dr. Moltmann's paper).

The specific way in which humanity is willed by God in a community of male and female reflects the image of God and constitutes the fulness of humanity. However, women in comparison to their male counterparts are often placed at a disadvantage through religious, legal, educational, and other factors. There is need for a positive program of study and action in the churches to eradicate all discrimination against women in church and society.

The differences in culture are in themselves normally neutral in relation to human rights, but cultural imperialism, or the abuse of cultural traditions, do endanger them. While no single culture can be normative for all, all are subject to the judgment of the Word of God if they violate the dignity of human beings.

b. *In relation to the State:*

It should be acknowledged that no human form of government is perfect, and all are necessarily under constant scrutiny in terms of the processes which they have promoted and do promote, and the processes which they counter and negate. As human rights are interrelated, and are also subject to ongoing historical processes, their fulfillment, negation, or violation by any group or agencies or even churches, has to be judged in a similar manner. Structures created by human beings are in constant danger of becoming self-perpetuating and self-fulfilling, and hence of becoming idols—in a truly biblical sense.

It should be observed that the Reformed tradition makes specific provision for the right and even the duty to resist, when human governments violate the purposes for which they were appointed. (Note the citations in Dr. Moltmann's paper.) The Christian community must be willing to become an offense to the powers in its support of the powerless and deprived. Christian resistance against oppressive powers is grounded in Christ's offering of his life for the redemption of the world (Phil. 2). It is thus the expression of the Christian's love for his neighbor, and not of self-concern. Our discipleship of Christ can take different forms in different situations:

—active and constructive resistance;
—passive resistance and civil disobedience;
—suffering and silent resistance;
—martyrdom.

c. *In relation to international affairs:*

Following the existing Covenants on Human Rights of 1966 there would seem to be the need for a further Human Rights' Covenant, a covenant relating to environmental rights. Such a covenant would be concerned with the responsible use of land and nature, and the capital resources of the world, the limitation within appropriate bounds of the development of industrial plants, and so on. These covenants have the value of functioning as continuing critiques of unjust situations.

Attention needs also to be given to the rights of future generations of the world, since there is the perpetual tendency to think in terms of the gratification of immediate needs, at the expense of those who will come after us.

The churches should take note of the escalation of violence and the development of destructive weapons in the world. It should be observed that "although there has been no direct military confrontation between the superpowers since World War II, some hundred wars have been fought, causing the deaths of more than ten million people in about sixty countries" (*The Armaments Situation,* WCC Fifth Assembly, 1975). These facts raise serious questions about any easy assumptions regarding just violence and unjust violence. The use of power to destroy people with apparent legality and impunity is a direct violation of that creation which has been made in the image of God and which has been called to live in the freedom of his grace.

3. Conclusion

As against the inclination on the part of many to shrink from this entire task because of its magnitude, it should be undertaken with hope. Because the responsibility for these concerns has been given by God they are not a mockery but are capable of fulfilment. No church, no Christian, no individual is powerless, but has a God-given competence, since "God has chosen the weak things of the world to confound the things that are mighty" (1 Cor. 1:27–29).

13. An Invitation to Study and Action

ALLEN O. MILLER

The foregoing pages incorporate a serious effort to deal with the issue of human rights from a Christian perspective. This marks the completion of a project initiated by the determination of the Uniting General Assembly of the World Alliance of Reformed Churches (Presbyterian and Congregational), convening in Nairobi, Kenya, in August 1970, to conduct an ecumenical study concerning "The Theological Basis of Human Rights and of the Liberation of Human Beings." It represents pioneering work on the part of the WARC Department of Theology, under the leadership of Jan Milič Lochman, and its two standing committees—the European Theological Commission and the North American Area Theological Committee. Appropriately, this body of essays, theses, and official documents is being presented on the occasion of the Centennial Consultation of the WARC, meeting in St. Andrews, Scotland, August 22–28, 1977.

Between Jürgen Moltmann's original study paper of 1971 and his definitive study paper of 1976, there are recorded here the carefully formulated responses of the two theological committees, along with a selection of the supporting papers originally written for their use. Those included were chosen because they face up to a variety of forms of human oppression (social, economic, cultural, ethnic, sexual) and because they represent several dimensions of approach to the human rights issue (philosophical, theological, spiritual, and political).

Finally, there are two sets of documents:

1. The United Nations *International Bill of Human Rights* (1948 and 1966), whose unfulfilled promises prompted the Alliance study in the first place, supplemented by the more recent Helsinki Agreement (1975) and "A Declaration of INTERdependence," by Henry Steele Commager.

Allen O. Miller, chairperson of the North American Area Theological Committee of the WARC, is professor of systematic theology and philosophy, Eden Theological Seminary, St. Louis.

2. The WARC's *Theological Basis of Human Rights*, including a set of theological guidelines and some practical implications, the report of the London Theological Consultation, February 18–21, 1976.

In commending the use of the WARC's "theological guidelines" with their "practical implications" to the churches in the English-speaking world, we are suggesting two things: first, that this collection be used as a sourcebook for serious study of the pressing issues of human rights, and secondly, that the churches and their individual members become intentionally involved in the struggle for the implementation of human rights in their own social, cultural, and political contexts.

A rising crescendo of concern about human rights—in Eastern Europe, the Soviet Union, Southern Africa, Northern Ireland, Chile, Korea, the Middle East, and North America—since the time when the report of the London Consultation was adopted in February 1976, indicates both the timeliness of the statement and the complexity of the issue, both within the church and in the world in which we live.

One cannot help being heartened and frightened by the timeliness of our study. The strong emphasis upon human rights in President Carter's inaugural address and cabinet appointments, the recent potentially creative and/or destructive tension between the USSR and the USA over human rights, the second round of meetings of the signatories of the Helsinki Agreement in June and September of 1977, the ambiguity inherent in the movements for black liberation in Southern Africa, the ambiguous, yes even tragic, conflict of human rights between the nation of Israel and the Palestinian Arabs, the parallel struggle of North American women for the right to ordination to the priesthood within the church and for an equal rights amendment to the Constitution of the United States—all this and more makes our study an example, par excellence, of Karl Barth's dictum regarding the need to keep the newspaper and the Bible in continuous living dialogue.

One thing is abundantly clear: there is no simple, much less simplistic, solution to the problems of inequity and injustice in human society. There is no fool-proof prescription for redressing human indignity and for freeing people from the bonds of oppression.

The struggle for a human right is—more often than not—countered not only by some human wrong, but also by some other human right. It is one thing to define which human rights are right, and quite another to achieve justice in the distribution of rights, *vis-à-vis* persons and groups, and in the determination of the jurisdiction within which such rights are assured—social or political, human or divine.

This book bears the title, *A Christian Declaration on Human Rights*. The deliberate juxtaposition of this title with the United Nations' Universal Declaration of Human Rights indicates at once the common concern and intention which they share and the point at which Christian faith adds a dimension which the United Nations' Universal Declaration cannot and does not have.

Let me try briefly to focus on that dimension and its significance. Christian faith and a broadly humanist faith both coalesce and divide on the issue of human rights. They coalesce on a common intention and goal—the freedom and dignity of human persons, with justice-in-community for all persons and peoples.[1] They divide appreciably both in theory and in practice.

[1] Cf. the remarkable parallel impact of a paragraph drawn from Henry Steele Commager's *A Declaration of INTERdependence* with the second (expanded) Guideline of the WARC's *Theological Basis of Human Rights:*

We hold these truths to be self-evident: that all men are created equal; that the inequalities and injustices which afflict so much of the human race are the product of history and society, not of God or nature; that people everywhere are entitled to the blessings of life and liberty, peace and security and the realization of their full potential; that they have an inescapable moral obligation to preserve those rights for posterity; and that to achieve these ends all the peoples and nations of the globe should acknowledge their interdependence and join together to dedicate their minds and their hearts to the solution of those problems which threaten their survival.

Our biblical faith commits us to a view of human life in its wholeness expressed in a matrix of basic complementarities:

body and soul
male and female
self and other
the individual and society
human life and its ecological context
religion and politics
time and eternity

In the identification of our humanity as created in the image of God, we affirm:

the equal worth and interdependence of body and soul in each person,
the equal dignity and interdependence of man and woman,
the equal validity and interdependence of personal rights (freedom and dignity) and social rights (justice and community), and
the equal dignity and interdependence of the present generation and future generations in the stewardship of nature.

As humanity stands in a covenant relationship to God, that relationship carries with it covenant responsibilities in our stewardship of creation.

153

Despite their common intention and goal, liberal humanism and Christian faith are engaging in two different processes. Liberalism is the source of a promethean effort to implement natural "human rights" in the course of human history. Christian faith bears witness to and bears the power of an historic event of "divine liberation."

The conceptuality of "human rights" arises out of the philosophy of the Enlightenment. As such, liberalism's view of being human is a secularized version of the biblical myth of humanity as being created in "the image of God." The "inalienable rights" with which human beings are said to be endowed are understood to be sustained by "the laws of Nature" and "Nature's God." Rooted in the philosophical assumption that being human is by Nature rational, this view rejects the correlative biblical myth of "the fall." Since it must, nevertheless, account for the sharp contrast between the potential and the actual in human life, liberalism has reified the transcendent dimension of "being human" into a permanent possession called "human rights," and has developed humanitarian movements for their implementation. This appears to be the only way a secular humanism can protect itself from cynical acquiescence in the obvious inequities which befall human life in natural history. Liberalism's principle of "human rights" is a promethean effort to save humanity from utter dehumanization and is more or less successful in its attempt.

This liberalism, which identifies human rights as natural and divinely bestowed and defines their basic expression as life, liberty, and the pursuit of property (happiness), has come to be the preeminent faith-claim of one quarter of the world—the dominating white minority which has its root in Europe and has been flowering there and in the Western hemisphere for three and more centuries. Its genius has been to foster republican government and the democratic process, literacy and liberal education, critical inquiry and scientific technology. It has spawned the capitalist economy and encouraged the

---

Bound by the claim of the great commandment (Mark 12:29–31), we acknowledge:

the equal worth and interdependence of one ethnic group and other ethnic groups in the totality of humanity,
the equal validity and interdependence of "my rights" and "the rights of my neighbour,"
the equal significance and interdependence of human rights and human duties, and
the equal claim and interdependence of religious faith and political responsibility in the life of the people of God.

practice of the self-determination of nations. In the name of this philosophy and its genius the predominately white peoples of European origin have claimed the whole world as their rightful domain. This goal has been achieved with remarkable effectiveness through four hundred years of white colonialism (territorial and cultural) and imperialism (military, political, and economic). At their hands, Third World peoples have suffered various forms of dehumanization—economic exploitation, political oppression, cultural genocide. Liberalism is the "promise" and "the abortion" of the *freedom* which is our human birthright and divine destiny.

The exercise of human rights is remarkably ambiguous: destructive as well as creative, demonic as well as holy. It is at best a tragic possibility for the elite and at worst a hellish nightmare for the great mass of human beings. Human rights participate fully in the ambiguity of human life as such. Being human is being threatened by the powers of evil, by Satan, sin, and death. These threats do not respect human rights, and human beings cry out for salvation!

It is the gospel confessed by Christians that the author of humanity and giver of his image, including the right to be human, is a "fellow-sufferer who understands." In Jesus Christ, the gracious Lord and sovereign lover of his creation promises and bestows salvation on his people. But salvation is multi-dimensional, correlative with the structures and dynamics which corrupt and negate human power, existence and life.

Satan is the negation of the power of being human, through the corruption of power itself. For the oppressed peoples of the earth Satan is the dominion of principalities and powers, oppressors pretending to represent the righteous lordship of God himself. Salvation from Satan is liberation from poverty, oppression, injustice, and the corruption of authority by its own pretension. *Christus Victor*, the righteous judge and king, is our Liberator and our hope for an age of justice and peace.

Sin is the negation of our existence through the corruption of faith by pretension. For oppressed peoples of the earth, sin means human sloth and irresponsibility. For their oppressors, sin means hybris—pride. For both, salvation is forgiveness, the rebirth of faith in the trustworthiness of God, being justified by grace for faith in Jesus as the Christ.

Death is the negation of life itself, the wages of sin, and the final enemy of everything finite. The gospel of salvation is eternal life, the miracle of new being through God's gracious action, the resurrection of the dead through the resurrection of the crucified Servant Jesus.

As the fourth theological guideline says, "We boldly confess the liberating power of Jesus Christ and affirm the Church's ministry of reconciliation and grace."

APPENDIXES

The United Nations International Bill of Human Rights

1. Universal Declaration of Human Rights

Adopted and proclaimed by General Assembly resolution 217 A (III) of 10 December 1948

Preamble

Whereas recognition of the inherent dignity and of the equal and inalienable rights of all members of the human family is the foundation of freedom, justice and peace in the world,

Whereas disregard and contempt for human rights have resulted in barbarous acts which have outraged the conscience of mankind, and the advent of a world in which human beings shall enjoy freedom of speech and belief and freedom from fear and want has been proclaimed as the highest aspiration of the common people,

Whereas it is essential, if man is not to be compelled to have recourse, as a last resort, to rebellion against tyranny and oppression, that human rights should be protected by the rule of law,

Whereas it is essential to promote the development of friendly relations between nations,

Whereas the peoples of the United Nations have in the Charter reaffirmed their faith in fundamental human rights, in the dignity and worth of the human person and in the equal rights of men and women and have determined to promote social progress and better standards of life in larger freedom,

Whereas Member States have pledged themselves to achieve, in co-operation with the United Nations, the promotion of universal respect for and observance of human rights and fundamental freedoms,

Whereas a common understanding of these rights and freedoms is of the greatest importance for the full realization of this pledge,

Now, therefore,
The General Assembly
Proclaims this Universal Declaration of Human Rights as a common standard of achievement for all peoples and all nations, to the end that every individual and every organ of society, keeping this Declaration constantly in mind, shall strive by teaching and education to promote respect for these rights and freedoms and by progressive measures, national and international, to secure their universal and effective recognition and observance, both among the peoples of Member States themselves and among the peoples of territories under their jurisdiction.

Article 1

All human beings are born free and equal in dignity and rights. They are endowed with reason and conscience and should act towards one another in a spirit of brotherhood.

Article 2

Everyone is entitled to all the rights and freedoms set forth in this Declaration, without distinction of any kind, such as race, colour, sex, language, religion, political or other opinion, national or social origin, property, birth or other status.

Furthermore, no distinction shall be made on the basis of the political, jurisdictional or international status of the country or territory to which a person belongs, whether it be independent, trust, non-self-governing or under any other limitation of sovereignty.

Article 3

Everyone has the right to life, liberty and the security of person.

Article 4

No one shall be held in slavery or servitude; slavery and the slave trade shall be prohibited in all their forms.

Article 5

No one shall be subjected to torture or to cruel, inhuman or degrading treatment or punishment.

Article 6

Everyone has the right to recognition everywhere as a person before the law.

Article 7

All are equal before the law and are entitled without any discrimination to equal protection of the law. All are entitled to equal protection against any discrimination in violation of this Declaration and against any incitement to such discrimination.

Article 8

Everyone has the right to an effective remedy by the competent national tribunals for acts violating the fundamental rights granted him by the constitution or by law.

Article 9

No one shall be subjected to arbitrary arrest, detention or exile.

Article 10

Everyone is entitled in full equality to a fair and public hearing by an independent and impartial tribunal, in the determination of his rights and obligations and of any criminal charge against him.

Article 11

1. Everyone charged with a penal offence has the right to be presumed innocent until proved guilty according to law in a public trial at which he has had all the guarantees necessary for his defence.

2. No one shall be held guilty of any penal offence on account of any act or omission which did not constitute a penal offence, under national or international law, at the time when it was commited. Nor shall a heavier penalty be imposed than the one that was applicable at the time the penal offence was committed.

Article 12

No one shall be subjected to arbitrary interference with his privacy, family, home or correspondence, nor to attacks upon his honour and reputation. Everyone has the right to the protection of the law against such interference or attacks.

Article 13

1. Everyone has the right to freedom of movement and residence within the borders of each State.

2. Everyone has the right to leave any country, including his own, and to return to his country.

Article 14

1. Everyone has the right to seek and to enjoy in other countries asylum from persecution.

2. This right may not be invoked in the case of prosecutions genuinely arising from non-political crimes or from acts contrary to the purposes and principles of the United Nations.

Article 15

1. Everyone has the right to a nationality.

2. No one shall be arbitrarily deprived of his nationality nor denied the right to change his nationality.

Article 16

1. Men and women of full age, without any limitation due to race, nationality or religion, have the right to marry and to found a family. They are entitled to equal rights as to marriage, during marriage and at its dissolution.

2. Marriage shall be entered into only with the free and full consent of the intending spouses.

3. The family is the natural and fundamental group unit of society and is entitled to protection by society and the State.

Article 17

1. Everyone has the right to own property alone as well as in association with others.

2. No one shall be arbitrarily deprived of his property.

Article 18

Everyone has the right to freedom of thought, conscience and religion; this right includes freedom to change his religion or belief, and freedom, either alone or in community with others and in public or private, to manifest his religion or belief in teaching, practice, worship and observance.

Article 19

Everyone has the right to freedom of opinion and expression; this right includes freedom to hold opinions without interference and to seek, receive and impart information and ideas through any media and regardless of frontiers.

Article 20

1. Everyone has the right to freedom of peaceful assembly and association.

2. No one may be compelled to belong to an association.

Article 21

1. Everyone has the right to take part in the government of his country, directly or through freely chosen representatives.
2. Everyone has the right of equal access to public service in his country.
3. The will of the people shall be the basis of the authority of government; this will shall be expressed in periodic and genuine elections which shall be by universal and equal suffrage and shall be held by secret vote or by equivalent free voting procedures.

Article 22

Everyone, as a member of society, has the right to social security and is entitled to realization, through national effort and international co-operation and in accordance with the organization and resources of each State, of the economic, social and cultural rights indispensable for his dignity and the free development of his personality.

Article 23

1. Everyone has the right to work, to free choice of employment, to just and favourable conditions of work and to protection against unemployment.
2. Everyone, without any discrimination, has the right to equal pay for equal work.
3. Everyone who works has the right to just and favourable remuneration ensuring for himself and his family an existence worthy of human dignity, and supplemented, if necessary, by other means of social protection.
4. Everyone has the right to form and to join trade unions for the protection of his interests.

Article 24

Everyone has the right to rest and leisure, including reasonable limitation of working hours and periodic holidays with pay.

Article 25

1. Everyone has the right to a standard of living adequate for the health and well-being of himself and of his family, including food, clothing, housing and medical care and necessary social services, and the right to security in the event of unemployment, sickness, disability, widowhood, old age or other lack of livelihood in circumstances beyond his control.

2. Motherhood and childhood are entitled to special care and assistance. All children, whether born in or out of wedlock, shall enjoy the same social protection.

Article 26

1. Everyone has the right to education. Education shall be free, at least in the elementary and fundamental stages. Elementary education shall be compulsory. Technical and professional education shall be made generally available and higher education shall be equally accessible to all on the basis of merit.

2. Education shall be directed to the full development of the human personality and to the strengthening of respect for human rights and fundamental freedoms. It shall promote understanding, tolerance and friendship among all nations, racial or religious groups, and shall further the activities of the United Nations for the maintenance of peace.

3. Parents have a prior right to choose the kind of education that shall be given to their children.

Article 27

1. Everyone has the right freely to participate in the cultural life of the community, to enjoy the arts and to share in scientific advancement and its benefits.

2. Everyone has the right to the protection of the moral and material interests resulting from any scientific, literary or artistic production of which he is the author.

Article 28

Everyone is entitled to a social and international order in which the rights and freedoms set forth in this Declaration can be fully realized.

Article 29

1. Everyone has duties to the community in which alone the free and full development of his personality is possible.

2. In the exercise of his rights and freedoms, everyone shall be subject only to such limitations as are determined by law solely for the purpose of securing due recognition and respect for the rights and freedoms of others and of meeting the just requirements of morality, public order and the general welfare in a democratic society.

3. These rights and freedoms may in no case be exercised contrary to the purposes and principles of the United Nations.

Article 30

Nothing in this Declaration may be interpreted as implying for any State, group or person any right to engage in any activity or to perform any act aimed at the destruction of any of the rights and freedoms set forth herein.

2. International Covenant on Economic, Social and Cultural Rights

Adopted and opened for signature, ratification and accession by General Assembly resolution 2200 A (XXI) of 16 December 1966

PREAMBLE

The States Parties to the present Covenant,

Considering that, in accordance with the principles proclaimed in the Charter of the United Nations, recognition of the inherent dignity and of the equal and inalienable rights of all members of the human family is the foundation of freedom, justice and peace in the world,

Recognizing that these rights derive from the inherent dignity of the human person,

Recognizing that, in accordance with the Universal Declaration of Human Rights, the ideal of free human beings enjoying freedom from fear and want can only be achieved if conditions are created whereby everyone may enjoy his economic, social and cultural rights, as well as his civil and political rights,

Considering the obligation of States under the Charter of the United Nations to promote universal respect for, and observance of, human rights and freedoms,

Realizing that the individual, having duties to other individuals and to the community to which he belongs, is under a responsibility, to strive for the promotion and observance of the rights recognized in the present Covenant,

Agree upon the following articles:

PART I

Article 1

1. All peoples have the right of self-determination. By virtue of that right they freely determine their political status and freely pursue their economic, social and cultural development.

2. All peoples may, for their own ends, freely dispose of their natural wealth and resources without prejudice to any obligations arising out of international economic co-operation, based upon the principle of mutual benefit, and international law. In no case may a people be deprived of its own means of subsistence.

3. The States Parties to the present Covenant, including those having responsibility for the administration of Non-Self-Governing and Trust Territories, shall promote the realization of the right of self-determination, and shall respect that right, in conformity with the provisions of the Charter of the United Nations.

PART II

Article 2

1. Each State Party to the present Covenant undertakes to take steps, individually and through international assistance and co-operation, especially economic and technical, to the maximum of its available resources, with a view to achieving progressively the full realization of the rights recognized in the present Covenant by all appropriate means, including particularly the adoption of legislative measures.

2. The States Parties to the present Covenant undertake to guarantee that the rights enunciated in the present Covenant will be exercised without discrimination of any kind as to race, colour, sex, language, religion, political or other opinion, national or social origin, property, birth or other status.

3. Developing countries, with due regard to human rights and their national economy, may determine to what extent they would guarantee the economic rights recognized in the present Covenant to non-nationals.

Article 3

The States Parties to the present Covenant undertake to ensure the equal right of men and women to the enjoyment of all economic, social and cultural rights set forth in the present Covenant.

Article 4

The States Parties to the present Covenant recognize that, in the enjoyment of those rights provided by the State in conformity with the present Covenant, the State may subject such rights only to such limitations as are determined by law only in so far as this may be compatible with the nature of these rights and solely for the purpose of promoting the general welfare in a democratic society.

Article 5

1. Nothing in the present Covenant may be interpteted as implying for any State, group or person any right to engage in any activity or to perform any act aimed at the destruction of any of the rights or freedoms recognized herein, or at their limitation to a greater extent than is provided for in the present Covenant.

2. No restriction upon or derogation from any of the fundamental human rights recognized or existing in any country in virtue of law, conventions, regulations or custom shall be admitted on the pretext that the present Covenant does not recognize such rights or that it recognizes them to a lesser extent.

PART III

Article 6

1. The States Parties to the present Covenant recognize the right to work, which includes the right of everyone to the opportunity to gain his living by work which he freely chooses or accepts, and will take appropriate steps to safeguard this right.

2. The steps to be taken by a State Party to the present Covenant to achieve the full realization of this right shall include technical and vocational guidance and training programmes, policies and techniques to achieve steady economic, social and cultural development and full and productive employment under conditions safeguarding fundamental political and economic freedoms to the individual.

Article 7

The States Parties to the present Covenant recognize the right of everyone to the enjoyment of just and favourable conditions of work which ensure, in particular:

(a) Remuneration which provides all workers, as a minimum, with:

(i) Fair wages and equal remuneration for work of equal value without distinction of any kind, in particular women being guaranteed conditions of work not inferi-

or to those enjoyed by men, with equal pay for equal work;

(ii) A decent living for themselves and their families in accordance with the provisions of the present Covenant;

(b) Safe and healthy working conditions;

(c) Equal opportunity for everyone to be promoted in his employment to an appropriate higher level, subject to no considerations other than those of seniority and competence;

(d) Rest, leisure and reasonable limitation of working hours and periodic holidays with pay, as well as remuneration for public holidays.

Article 8

1. The States Parties to the present Covenant undertake to ensure:

(a) The right of everyone to form trade unions and join the trade union of his choice, subject only to the rules of the organization concerned, for the promotion and protection of his economic and social interests. No restrictions may be placed on the exercise of this right other than those prescribed by law and which are necessary in a democratic society in the interests of national security or public order or for the protection of the rights and freedoms of others;

(b) The right of trade unions to establish national federations or confederations and the right of the latter to form or join international trade-union organizations;

(c) The right of trade unions to function freely subject to no limitations other than those prescribed by law and which are necessary in a democratic society in the interests of national security or public order or for the protection of the rights and freedoms of others;

(d) The right to strike, provided that it is exercised in conformity with the laws of the particular country.

2. This article shall not prevent the imposition of lawful restrictions on the exercise of these rights by members of the armed forces or of the police or of the administration of the State.

3. Nothing in this article shall authorize States Parties to the International Labour Organisation Convention of 1948 concerning Freedom of Association and Protection of the Right to Organize to take legislative measures which would prejudice, or apply the law in such a manner as would prejudice, the guarantees provided for in that Convention.

Article 9

The States Parties to the present Covenant recognize the right of everyone to social security, including social insurance.

Article 10

The States Parties to the present Covenant recognize that:

1. The widest possible protection and assistance should be accorded to the family, which is the natural and fundamental group unit of society, particularly for its establishment and while it is responsible for the care and education of dependent children. Marriage must be entered into with the free consent of the intending spouses.

2. Special protection should be accorded to mothers during a reasonable period before and after childbirth. During such period working mothers should be accorded paid leave or leave with adequate social security benefits.

3. Special measures of protection and assistance should be taken on behalf of all children and young persons without any discrimination for reasons of parentage or other conditions. Children and young persons should be protected from economic and social exploitation. Their employment in work harmful to their morals or health or dangerous to life or likely to hamper their normal development should be punishable by law. States should also set age limits below which the paid employment of child labour should be prohibited and punishable by law.

Article 11

1. The States Parties to the present Covenant recognize the right of everyone to an adequate standard of living for himself and his family, including adequate food, clothing and housing, and to the continuous improvement of living conditions. The States Parties will take appropriate steps to ensure the realization of this right, recognizing to this effect the essential importance of international co-operation based on free consent.

2. The States Parties of the present Covenant, recognizing the fundamental right of everyone to be free from hunger, shall take, individually and through international co-operation, the measures, including specific programmes, which are needed:

(a) To improve methods of production, conservation and distribution of food by making full use of technical and scientific knowledge, by disseminating knowledge of the principles of nutrition and by developing or reforming agrarian systems in such a way as to achieve the most efficient development and utilization of natural resources;

(b) Taking into account the problems of both food-importing and food-exporting countries, to ensure an equitable distribution of world food supplies in relation to need.

Article 12

1. The States Parties to the present Covenant recognize the right of everyone to the enjoyment of the highest attainable standard of physical and mental health.

2. The steps to be taken by the States Parties to the present Covenant to achieve the full realization of this right shall include those necessary for:

(a) The provision for the reduction of the stillbirth-rate and of infant mortality and for the healthy development of the child;

(b) The improvement of all aspects of environmental and industrial hygiene;

(c) The prevention, treatment and control of epidemic, endemic, occupational and other diseases;

(d) The creation of conditions which would assure to all medical service and medical attention in the event of sickness.

Article 13

1. The States Parties to the present Covenant recognize the right of everyone to education. They agree that education shall be directed to the full development of the human personality and the sense of its dignity, and shall strengthen the respect for human rights and fundamental freedoms. They further agree that education shall enable all persons to participate effectively in a free society, promote understanding, tolerance and friendship among all nations and all racial, ethnic or religious groups, and further the activities of the United Nations for the maintenance of peace.

2. The States Parties to the present Covenant recognize that, with a view to achieving the full realization of this right:

(a) Primary education shall be compulsory and available free to all;

(b) Secondary education in its different forms, including technical and vocational secondary education, shall be made generally available and accessible to all by every appropriate means, and in particular by the progressive introduction of free education;

(c) Higher education shall be made equally accessible to all, on the basis of capacity, by every appropriate means, and in particular by the progressive introduction of free education;

(d) Fundamental education shall be encouraged or intensified as far as possible for those persons who have not received or completed the whole period of their primary education;

(e) The development of a system of schools at all levels shall be actively pursued, an adequate fellowship system shall be established, and the material conditions of teaching staff shall be continuously improved.

3. The States Parties to the present Covenant undertake to have respect for the liberty of parents and, when applicable, legal guardians to choose for their children schools, other than those established by the public authorities, which conform to such minimum educational standards as may be laid down or approved by the State and to ensure the religious and moral education of their children in conformity with their own convictions.

4. No part of this article shall be construed so as to interfere with the liberty of individuals and bodies to establish and direct educational institutions, subject always to the observance of the principles set forth in paragraph 1 of this article and to the requirement that the education given in such institutions shall conform to such minimum standards as may be laid down by the State.

Article 14

Each State Party to the present Covenant which, at the time of becoming a Party, has not been able to secure in its metropolitan territory or other territories under its jurisdiction compulsory primary education, free of charge, undertakes, within two years, to work out and adopt a detailed plan of action for the progressive implementation, within a reasonable number of years, to be fixed in the plan, of the principle of compulsory education free of charge for all.

Article 15

1. The States Parties to the present Covenant recognize the right of everyone:

(a) To take part in cultural life;

(b) To enjoy the benefits of scientific progress and its applications;

(c) To benefit from the protection of the moral and material interests resulting from any scientific, literary or artistic production of which he is the author.

2. The steps to be taken by the States Parties to the present Covenant to achieve the full realization of this right shall include those necessary for the conservation, the development and the diffusion of science and culture.

3. The States Parties to the present Covenant undertake to respect the freedom indispensable for scientific research and creative activity.

4. The States Parties to the present Covenant recognize the benefits to be derived from the encouragement and development of international contacts and co-operation in the scientific and cultural fields.

3. International Covenant on Civil and Political Rights

Adopted and opened for signature, ratification and accession by General Assembly resolution 2200 A (XXI) of 16 December 1966

PREAMBLE

The States Parties to the present Covenant,

Considering that, in accordance with the principles proclaimed in the Charter of the United Nations recognition of the inherent dignity and of the equal and inalienable rights of all members of the human family is the foundation of freedom, justice and peace in the world,

Recognizing that these rights derive from the inherent dignity of the human person,

Recognizing that, in accordance with the Universal Declaration of Human Rights, the ideal of free human beings enjoying civil and political freedom and freedom from fear and want can only be achieved if conditions are created whereby everyone may enjoy his civil and political rights, as well as his economic, social and cultural rights,

Considering the obligation of States under the Charter of the United Nations to promote universal respect for, and observance of, human rights and freedoms,

Realizing that the individual, having duties to other individuals and to the community to which he belongs, is under a responsibility to strive for the promotion and observance of the rights recognized in the present Covenant,

Agree upon the following articles:

PART I

Article 1

1. All peoples have the right of self-determination. By virtue of that right they freely determine their political status and freely pursue their economic, social and cultural development.

2. All peoples may, for their own ends, freely dispose of their natural wealth and resources without prejudice to any obligations arising out of international economic co-operation, based upon the principle of mutual benefit, and international law. In no case may a people be deprived of its own means of subsistence.

3. The States Parties to the present Covenant, including those having responsibility for the administration of Non-Self-Governing and Trust Territories, shall promote the realization of the right of self-determination, and shall respect that right, in conformity with the provisions of the Charter of the United Nations.

PART II

Article 2

1. Each State Party to the present Covenant undertakes to respect and to ensure to all individuals within its territory and subject to its jurisdiction the rights recognized in the present Covenant, without distinction of any kind, such as race, colour, sex, language, religion, political or other opinion, national or social origin, property, birth or other status.

2. Where not already provided for by existing legislative or other measures, each State Party to the present Covenant undertakes to take the necessary steps, in accordance with its constitutional processes and with the provisions of the present Covenant, to adopt such legislative or other measures as may be necessary to give effect to the rights recognized in the present Covenant.

3. Each State Party to the present Covenant undertakes:

(*a*) To ensure that any person whose rights or freedoms as herein recognized are violated shall have an effective remedy, notwithstanding that the violation has been committed by persons acting in an official capacity;

(*b*) To ensure that any person claiming such a remedy shall have his right thereto determined by competent judicial, administrative or legislative authorities, or by any other com-

173

petent authority provided for by the legal system of the State, and to develop the possibilities of judicial remedy;

(c) To ensure that the competent authorities shall enforce such remedies when granted.

Article 3

The States Parties to the present Covenant undertake to ensure the equal right of men and women to the enjoyment of all civil and political rights set forth in the present Covenant.

Article 4

1. In the time of public emergency which threatens the life of the nation and the existence of which is officially proclaimed, the States Parties to the present Covenant may take measures derogating from their obligations under the present Covenant to the extent strictly required by the exigencies of the situation, provided that such measures are not inconsistent with their other obligations under international law and do not involve discrimination solely on the ground of race, colour, sex, language, religion or social origin.

2. No derogation from articles 6, 7, 8 (paragraphs 1 and 2), 11, 15, 16 and 18 may be made under this provision.

3. Any State Party to the present Covenant availing itself of the right of derogation shall immediately inform the other States Parties to the present Covenant, through the intermediary of the Secretary-General of the United Nations, of the provisions from which it has derogated and of the reasons by which it was actuated. A further communication shall be made, through the same intermediary, on the date on which it terminates such derogation.

Article 5

1. Nothing in the present Covenant may be interpreted as implying for any State, group or person any right to engage in any activity or perform any act aimed at the destruction of any of the rights and freedoms recognized herein or at their limitation to a greater extent than is provided for in the present Covenant.

2. There shall be no restriction upon or derogation from any of the fundamental human rights recognized or existing in any State Party to the present Covenant pursuant to law, conventions, regulations or custom on the pretext that the present Covenant does not recognize such rights or that it recognizes them to a lesser extent.

PART III

Article 6

1. Every human being has the inherent right to life. This right shall be protected by law. No one shall be arbitrarily deprived of his life.

2. In countries which have not abolished the death penalty, sentence of death may be imposed only for the most serious crimes in accordance with the law in force at the time of the commission of the crime and not contrary to the provisions of the present Covenant and to the Convention on the Prevention and Punishment of the Crime of Genocide. This penalty can only be carried out pursuant to a final judgment rendered by a competent court.

3. When deprivation of life constitutes the crime of genocide, it is understood that nothing in this article shall authorize any State Party to the present Covenant to derogate in any way from any obligation assumed under the provisions of the Convention on the Prevention and Punishment of the Crime of Genocide.

4. Anyone sentenced to death shall have the right to seek pardon or commutation of the sentence. Amnesty, pardon or commutation of the sentence of death may be granted in all cases.

5. Sentence of death shall not be imposed for crimes committed by persons below eighteen years of age and shall not be carried out on pregnant women.

6. Nothing in this article shall be invoked to delay or to prevent the abolition of capital punishment by any State Party to the present Covenant.

Article 7

No one shall be subjected to torture or to cruel, inhuman or degrading treatment or punishment. In particular, no one shall be subjected without his free consent to medical or scientific experimentation.

Article 8

1. No one shall be held in slavery; slavery and the slave-trade in all their forms shall be prohibited.

2. No one shall be held in servitude.

3. (a) No one shall be required to perform forced or compulsory labour;

(b) Paragraph 3 (a) shall not be held to preclude, in countries where imprisonment with hard labour may be imposed as a punishment for a crime, the performance of hard labour in pursuance of a sentence to such punishment by a competent court;

(c) For the purpose of this paragraph the term "forced or compulsory labour" shall not include:

(i) Any work or service, not referred to in subparagraph (b), normally required of a person who is under detention in consequence of a lawful order of a court, or of a person during conditional release from such detention;

(ii) Any service of a military character and, in countries where conscientious objection is recognized, any national service required by law of conscientious objectors;

(iii) Any service exacted in cases of emergency or calamity threatening the life or well-being of the community;

(iv) Any work or service which forms part of normal civil obligations.

Article 9

1. Everyone has the right to liberty and security of person. No one shall be subjected to arbitrary arrest or detention. No one shall be deprived of his liberty except on such grounds and in accordance with such procedure as are established by law.

2. Anyone who is arrested shall be informed, at the time of arrest, of the reasons for his arrest and shall be promptly informed of any charges against him.

3. Anyone arrested or detained on a criminal charge shall be brought promptly before a judge or other officer authorized by law to exercise judicial power and shall be entitled to trial within a reasonable time or to release. It shall not be the general rule that persons awaiting trial shall be detained in custody, but release may be subject to guarantees to appear for trial, at any other stage of the judicial proceedings, and, should occasion arise, for execution of the judgement.

4. Anyone who is deprived of his liberty by arrest or detention shall be entitled to take proceedings before a court, in order that that court may decide without delay on the lawfulness of his detention and order his release if the detention is not lawful.

5. Anyone who has been the victim of unlawful arrest or detention shall have an enforceable right to compensation.

Article 10

1. All persons deprived of their liberty shall be treated with humanity and with respect for the inherent dignity of the human person.

2. (*a*) Accused persons shall, save in exceptional circumstances, be segregated from convicted persons and shall be subject to separate treatment appropriate to their status as unconvicted persons;

(*b*) Accused juvenile persons shall be separated from adults and brought as speedily as possible for adjudication.

3. The penitentiary system shall comprise treatment of prisoners the essential aim of which shall be their reformation and social rehabilitation. Juvenile offenders shall be segregated from adults and be accorded treatment appropriate to their age and legal status.

Article 11

No one shall be imprisoned merely on the ground of inability to fulfil a contractual obligation.

Article 12

1. Everyone lawfully within the territory of a State shall, within that territory, have the right to liberty of movement and freedom to choose his residence.

2. Everyone shall be free to leave any country, including his own.

3. The above-mentioned rights shall not be subject to any restrictions except those which are provided by law, are necessary to protect national security, public order (*ordre public*), public health or morals or the rights and freedoms of others, and are consistent with the other rights recognized in the present Covenant.

4. No one shall be arbitrarily deprived of the right to enter his own country.

Article 13

An alien lawfully in the territory of a State Party to the present Covenant may be expelled therefrom only in pursuance of a decision reached in accordance with law and shall, except where compelling reasons of national security otherwise require, be allowed to submit the reasons against his expulsion and to have his case reviewed by, and be represented for the purpose before, the competent authority or a person or persons especially designated by the competent authority.

Article 14

1. All persons shall be equal before the courts and tribunals. In the determination of any criminal charge against him, or of his rights and obligations in a suit at law, everyone shall be entitled to a fair and public hearing by a competent, independent and impartial tribunal established by law. The Press and the public may be excluded from all or part of a trial for reasons of morals, public order (*ordre public*) or national security in a democratic society, or when the interest of the private lives of the parties so requires, or to the extent strictly necessary in the opinion of the court in special circumstances where publicity would prejudice the interests of justice; but any judgement rendered in a criminal case or in a suit at law shall be made public except where the interest of juvenile persons otherwise requires or the proceedings concern matrimonial disputes or the guardianship of children.

2. Everyone charged with a criminal offence shall have the right to be presumed innocent until proved guilty according to law.

3. In the determination of any criminal charge against him, everyone shall be entitled to the following minimum guarantees, in full equality:

(*a*) To be informed promptly and in detail in a language which he understands of the nature and cause of the charge against him;

(*b*) To have adequate time and facilities for the preparation of his defence and to communicate with counsel of his own choosing;

(*c*) To be tried without undue delay;

(*d*) To be tried in his presence, and to defend himself in person or through legal assistance of his own choosing; to be informed, if he does not have legal assistance, of this right; and to have legal assistance assigned to him, in any case where the interests of justice so require, and without payment by him in any such case if he does not have sufficient means to pay for it;

(*e*) To examine, or have examined, the witnesses against him and to obtain the attendance and examination of witnesses on his behalf under the same conditions as witnesses against him;

(*f*) To have the free assistance of an interpreter if he cannot understand or speak the language used in court;

(*g*) Not to be compelled to testify against himself or to confess guilt.

4. In the case of juvenile persons, the procedure shall be such as will take account of their age and the desirability of promoting their rehabilitation.

5. Everyone convicted of a crime shall have the right to his conviction and sentence being reviewed by a higher tribunal according to law.

6. When a person has by a final decision been convicted of a criminal offence and when subsequently his conviction has been reversed or he has been pardoned on the ground that a new or newly discovered fact shows conclusively that there has been a miscarriage of justice, the person who has suffered punishment as a result of such conviction shall be compensated according to law, unless it is proved that the non-disclosure of the unknown fact in time is wholly or partly attributable to him.

7. No one shall be liable to be tried or punished again for an offence for which he has already been finally convicted or acquitted in accordance with the law and penal procedure of each country.

Article 15

1. No one shall be held guilty of any criminal offence on account of any act or omission which did not constitute a criminal offence, under national or international law, at the time when it was committed. Nor shall a heavier penalty be imposed than the one that was applicable at the time when the criminal offence was committed. If, subsequent to the commission of the offence, provision is made by law for the imposition of the lighter penalty, the offender shall benefit thereby.

2. Nothing in this article shall prejudice the trial and punishment of any person for any act or omission which, at the time when it was committed, was criminal according to the general principles of law recognized by the community of nations.

Article 16

Everyone shall have the right to recognition everywhere as a person before the law.

Article 17

1. No one shall be subjected to arbitrary or unlawful interference with his privacy, family, home or correspondence, nor to unlawful attacks on his honour and reputation.

2. Everyone has the right to the protection of the law against such interference or attacks.

Article 18

1. Everyone shall have the right to freedom of thought, conscience and religion. This right shall include freedom to have or to adopt a religion or belief of his choice, and freedom, either individually or in community with others and in public or private, to manifest his religion or belief in worship, observance, practice and teaching.

2. No one shall be subject to coercion which would impair his freedom to have or to adopt a religion or belief of his choice.

3. Freedom to manifest one's religion or beliefs may be subject only to such limitations as are prescribed by law and are necessary to protect public safety, order, health, or morals or the fundamental rights and freedoms of others.

4. The States Parties to the present Covenant undertake to have respect for the liberty of parents and, when applicable, legal guardians to ensure the religious and moral education of their children in conformity with their own convictions.

Article 19

1. Everyone shall have the right to hold opinions without interference.

2. Everyone shall have the right to freedom of expression; this right shall include freedom to seek, receive and impart information and ideas of all kinds, regardless of frontiers, either orally, in writing or in print, in the form of art, of through any other media of his choice.

3. The exercise of the rights provided for in paragraph 2 of this article carries with it special duties and responsibilities. It may therefore be subject to certain restrictions, but these shall only be such as are provided by law and are necessary:

(a) For respect of the rights or reputations of others;

(b) For the protection of national security or of public order (*ordre public*), or of public health or morals.

Article 20

1. Any propaganda for war shall be prohibited by law.

2. Any advocacy of national, racial or religious hatred that constitutes incitement to discrimination, hostility or violence shall be prohibited by law.

Article 21

The right of peaceful assembly shall be recognized. No restrictions may be placed on the exercise of this right other than those imposed in conformity with the law and which are necessary in a democratic society in the interests of national security or public safety, public order (*ordre public*), the protection of public health or morals or the protection of the rights and freedoms of others.

Article 22

1. Everyone shall have the right to freedom of association with others, including the right to form and join trade unions for the protection of his interests.

2. No restrictions may be placed on the exercise of this right other than those which are prescribed by law and which are necessary in a democratic society in the interests of national security or public safety, public order (*ordre public*), the protection of public health or morals or the protection of the rights and freedoms of others. This article shall not prevent the imposition of lawful restrictions on members of the armed forces and of the police in their exercise of this right.

3. Nothing in this article shall authorize States Parties to the International Labour Organisation Convention of 1948 concerning Freedom of Association and Protection of the Right to Organize to take legislative measures which would prejudice, or to apply the law in such a manner as to prejudice the guarantees provided for in that Convention.

Article 23

1. The family is the natural and fundamental group unit of society and is entitled to protection by society and the State.

2. The right of men and women of marriageable age to marry and to found a family shall be recognized.

3. No marriage shall be entered into without the free and full consent of the intending spouses.

4. States Parties to the present Covenant shall take appropriate steps to ensure equality of rights and responsibilities of spouses as to marriage, during marriage and at its dissolution. In the case of dissolution, provision shall be made for the necessary protection of any children.

Article 24

1. Every child shall have, without discrimination as to race, colour, sex, language, religion, national or social origin, prop-

erty or birth, the right to such measures of protection as are required by his status as a minor, on the part of his family, society and the State.

2. Every child shall be registered immediately after birth and shall have a name.

3. Every child has the right to acquire a nationality.

Article 25

Every citizen shall have the right and the opportunity, without any of the distinctions mentioned in article 2 and without unreasonable restrictions:

(*a*) To take part in the conduct of public affairs, directly or through freely chosen representations.

(*b*) To vote and to be elected at genuine periodic elections which shall be by universal and equal suffrage and shall be held by secret ballot, guaranteeing the free expression of the will of the electors;

(*c*) To have access, on general terms of equality, to public service in his country.

Article 26

All persons are equal before the law and are entitled without any discrimination to the equal protection of the law. In this respect, the law shall prohibit any discrimination and guarantee to all persons equal and effective protection against discrimination on any ground such as race, colour, sex, language, religion, political or other opinion, national or social origin, property, birth or other status.

Article 27

In those States in which ethnic, religious or linguistic minorities exist, persons belonging to such minorities shall not be denied the right, in community with the other members of their group, to enjoy their own culture, to profess and practice their own religion, or to use their own language.

The Helsinki Agreement

Principle VII (guiding relations between Participating States) Respect for Human Rights and Fundamental Freedoms, Including the Freedom of Thought, Conscience, Religion, or Belief

The participating States will respect human rights and fundamental freedoms, including the freedom of thought, conscience, religion or belief, for all without distinction as to race, sex, language or religion.

They will promote and encourage the effective exercise of civil, political, economic, social, cultural and other rights and freedoms all of which derive from the inherent dignity of the human person and are essential for his free and full development.

Within this framework the participating States will recognize and respect the freedom of the individual to profess and practise, alone or in community with others, religion or belief acting in accordance with the dictates of his own conscience.

The participating States on whose territory national minorities exist will respect the right of persons belonging to such minorities to equality before the law, will afford them the full opportunity for the actual enjoyment of human rights and fundamental freedoms and will, in this manner, protect their legitimate interests in this sphere.

The participating States recognize the universal significance of human rights and fundamental freedoms, respect for which is an essential factor for the peace, justice and well-being necessary to ensure the development of friendly relations and co-operation among themselves as among all States.

These excerpts are from the final act of the Conference on Security and Cooperation in Europe. The Agreement was signed on August 1, 1975, in Helsinki by 33 European states, the USA, and Canada.

They will constantly respect these rights and freedoms in their mutual relations and will endeavour jointly and separately, including in co-operation with the United Nations, to promote universal and effective respect for them. They confirm the right of the individual to know and act upon his rights and duties in this field.

In the field of human rights and fundamental freedoms, the participating States will act in conformity with the purposes and principles of the Charter of the United Nations and with the Universal Declaration of Human Rights. They will also fulfil their obligations as set forth in the international declarations and agreements in this field, including inter alia the International Covenants on Human Rights, by which they may be bound.

Co-operation in Humanitarian and Other Fields

The participating States:

Desiring to contribute to the strengthening of peace and understanding among peoples and to the spiritual enrichment of the human personality without distinction as to race, sex, language or religion,

Conscious that increased cultural and educational exchanges, broader dissemination of information, contacts between people, and the solution of humanitarian problems will contribute to the attainment of these aims,

Determined therefore to co-operate among themselves, irrespective of their political, economic and social systems, in order to create better conditions in the above fields, to develop and strengthen existing forms of co-operation and to work out new ways and means appropriate to these aims,

Convinced that this co-operation should take place in full respect for the principles guiding relations among participating States as set forth in the relevant document,

Have adopted the following:

1. Human Contacts

The participating States,

Considering the development of contacts to be an important element in the strengthening of friendly relations and trust among peoples,

Affirming, in relation to their present effort to improve conditions in this area, the importance they attach to humanitarian considerations,

Desiring in this spirit to develop, with the continuance of détente, further efforts to achieve continuing progress in this field,

And conscious that the question relevant hereto must be settled by the States concerned under mutually acceptable conditions,

Make it their aim to facilitate freer movement and contacts, individually and collectively, whether privately or officially, among persons, institutions and organizations of the participating States, and to contribute to the solution of the humanitarian problems that arise in that connexion,

Declare their readiness to these ends to take measures which they consider appropriate and to conclude agreements or arrangements among themselves, as may be needed, and

Express their intention now to proceed to the implementation of the following:

(a) *Contacts and Regular Meetings on the Basis of Family Ties*

In order to promote further development of contacts on the basis of family ties the participating States will favourably consider applications for travel with the purpose of allowing persons to enter or leave their territory temporarily, and on a regular basis if desired, in order to visit members of their families.

Applications for temporary visits to meet members of their families will be dealt with without distinction as to the country of origin or destination; existing requirements for travel documents and visas will be applied in the spirit. The preparation and issue of such documents and visas will be effected within reasonable time limits; cases of urgent necessity—such as serious illness or death—will be given priority treatment. They will take such steps as may be necessary to ensure that the fees for official travel documents and visas are acceptable.

They confirm that the presentation of an application concerning contacts on the basis of family ties will not modify the rights and obligations of the applicant or of members of his family.

(b) *Reunification of Families*

The participating States will deal in a positive and humanitarian spirit with the applications of persons who wish to be reunited with members of their family, with special attention being given to requests of an urgent character—such as requests submitted by persons who are ill or old.

185

They will deal with applications in this field as expeditiously as possible.

They will lower where necessary the fees charged in connexion with these applications to ensure that they are at a moderate level.

Applications for the purpose of family reunification which are not granted may be renewed at the appropriate level and will be reconsidered at reasonably short intervals by the authorities of the country of residence or destination, whichever is concerned; under such circumstances fees will be charged only when applications are granted.

Persons whose applications for family reunification are granted may bring with them or ship their household and personal effects; to this end the participating States will use all possibilities provided by existing regulations.

Until members of the same family are reunited meetings and contacts between them may take place in accordance with the modalities for contacts on the basis of family ties.

The participating States will support the efforts of Red Cross and Red Crescent Societies concerned with the problems of family reunification.

They confirm that the presentation of an application concerning family reunification will not modify the rights and obligations of the applicant or of members of his family.

The receiving participating State will take appropriate care with regard to employment for persons from other participating States who take up permanent residence in that State in connexion with family reunification with its citizens and see that they are afforded opportunities equal to those enjoyed by its own citizens for education, medical assistance and social security.

(c) *Marriage between Citizens of Different States*

The participating States will examine favourably and on the basis of humanitarian considerations requests for exit or entry permits from persons who have decided to marry a citizen from another participating State.

The processing and issuing of the documents required for the above purposes and for the marriage will be in accordance with the provisions accepted for family reunification.

In dealing with requests from couples from different participating States, once married, to enable them and the minor children of their marriage to transfer their permanent residence to a State in which either one is normally a resident, the participating States will also apply the provisions accepted for family reunification.

(d) *Travel for Personal or Professional Reasons*

The participating States intend to facilitate wider travel by their citizens for personal or professional reasons and to this end they intend in particular:

—gradually to simplify and to administer flexibly the procedures for exit and entry;

—to ease regulations concerning movement of citizens from the other participating States in their territory, with due regard to security requirements.

They will endeavour gradually to lower, where necessary, the fees for visas and official travel documents.

They intend to consider, as necessary, means—including, insofar as appropriate, the conclusion of multilateral or bilateral consular conventions or other relevant agreements or understandings—for the improvement of arrangements to provide consular services, including legal and consular assistance.

* * * * *

They confirm that religious faiths, institutions and organizations, practising within the constitutional framework of the participating States, and their representatives can, in the field of their activities, have contacts and meetings among themselves and exchange information.

A Declaration of INTERdependence

HENRY STEELE COMMAGER

When in the course of history the threat of extinction confronts mankind, it is necessary for the people of The United States to declare their interdependence with the people of all nations and to embrace those principles and build those institutions which will enable mankind to survive and civilization to flourish.

Two centuries ago our forefathers brought forth a new nation; now we must join with others to bring forth a new world order. On this historic occasion it is proper that the American people should reaffirm those principles on which the United States of America was founded, acknowledge the new crises which confront them, accept the new obligations which history imposes upon them, and set forth the causes which impel them to affirm before all peoples their commitment to a Declaration of Interdependence.

We hold these truths to be self-evident: that all men are created equal; that the inequalities and injustices which afflict so much of the human race are the product of history and society, not of God or nature; that people everywhere are entitled to the blessings of life and liberty, peace and security and the realization of their full potential; that they have an inescapable moral obligation to preserve those rights for posterity; and that to achieve these ends all the peoples and nations of the globe should acknowledge their interdependence and join together to dedicate their minds and their hearts to the solution of those problems which threaten their survival.

To establish a new world order of compassion, peace, justice and security, it is essential that mankind free itself from the limitations of national prejudice, and acknowledge that the forces that unite it are incomparably deeper than those that

Public Affairs Council of Philadelphia, 1975.

divide it—that all people are part of one global community, dependent on one body of resources, bound together by the ties of a common humanity and associated in a common adventure on the planet Earth.

Let us then join together to vindicate and realize this great truth that mankind is one, and as one will nobly save or irreparably lose the heritage of thousands of years of civilization. And let us set forth the principles which should animate and inspire us if our civilization is to survive.

WE AFFIRM that the resources of the globe are finite, not infinite, that they are the heritage of no one nation or generation, but of all peoples, nations and of posterity, and that our deepest obligation is to transmit to that posterity a planet richer in material bounty, in beauty and in delight than we found it. Narrow notions of national sovereignty must not be permitted to curtail that obligation.

WE AFFIRM that the exploitation of the poor by the rich, and the weak by the strong violates our common humanity and denies to large segments of society the blessings of life, liberty and happiness. We recognize a moral obligation to strive for a more prudent and more equitable sharing of the resources of the earth in order to ameliorate poverty, hunger and disease.

WE AFFIRM that the resources of nature are sufficient to nourish and sustain all the present inhabitants of the globe and that there is an obligation on every society to distribute those resources equitably, along with a corollary obligation upon every society to assure that its population does not place upon Nature a burden heavier than it can bear.

WE AFFIRM our responsibility to help create conditions which will make for peace and security and to build more effective machinery for keeping peace among the nations. Because the insensate accumulation of nuclear, chemical and biological weapons threatens the survival of Mankind we call for the immediate reduction and eventual elimination of these weapons under international supervision. We deplore the reliance on force to settle disputes between nation states and between rival groups within such states.

WE AFFIRM that the oceans are the common property of mankind whose dependence on their incomparable resources of nourishment and strength will, in the next century, become crucial for human survival, and that their exploitation should be so regulated as to serve the interests of the entire globe, and of future generations.

WE AFFIRM that pollution flows with the waters and flies with the winds, that it recognizes no boundary lines and penetrates all defenses, that it works irreparable damage alike to Nature and to Mankind—threatening with extinction the life of the seas, the flora and fauna of the earth, the health of the people in cities and the countryside alike—and that it can be adequately controlled only through international cooperation.

WE AFFIRM that the exploration and utilization of outer space is a matter equally important to all the nations of the globe and that no nation can be permitted to exploit or develop the potentialities of the planetary system exclusively for its own benefit.

WE AFFIRM that the economy of all nations is a seamless web, and that no one nation can any longer effectively maintain its processes of production and monetary systems without recognizing the necessity for collaborative regulation by international authorities.

WE AFFIRM that in a civilized society, the institutions of science and the arts are never at war and call upon all nations to exempt these institutions from the claims of chauvinistic nationalism and to foster that great community of learning and creativity whose benign function is to advance civilization and the health and happiness of mankind.

WE AFFIRM that a world without law is a world without order, and we call upon all nations to strengthen and to sustain the United Nations and its specialized agencies, and other institutions of world order, and to broaden the jurisdiction of the World Court, that these may preside over a reign of law that will not only end wars but end as well that mindless violence which terrorizes our society even in times of peace.

We can no longer afford to make little plans, allow ourselves to be the captives of events and forces over which we have no control, consult our fears rather than our hopes. We call upon the American people, on the threshold of the third century of their national existence, to display once again that boldness, enterprise, magnanimity and vision which enabled the founders of our Republic to bring forth a new nation and inaugurate a new era in human history. The fate of humanity hangs in the balance. Throughout the globe, hearts and hopes wait upon us. We summon all Mankind to unite to meet the great challenge.